Circling The Drain

A Story Of Hope, Lost Children, And Finding Home

Kimberly A. Luse

Anne —
always let love
lead you home —
Kimberly

1

ISBN-13: 978-1985389618

ISBN-10: 1985389614

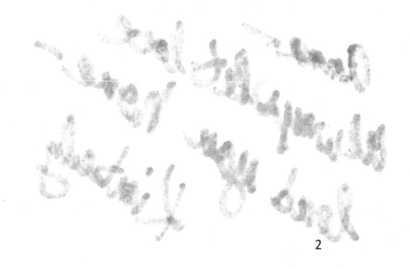

Dedicated to my mother, my first and greatest
teacher

Table of Contents

Preface...............7

Chapter 1 (1969) Jax, Jumping Rope, and Wetting Your Pants...........11

Chapter 2 (1971) Finding Jesus and Losing Myself...............19

Chapter 3 (1975) Cover Girl and Hiding............27

Chapter 4 (1977) On Fire: Beverly Hills and Leo 33

Chapter 5 (1978) The Newport Girl 41

Chapter 6 (1980) Waiting for a Girl Like You and Grilled Cheese Sandwiches..............53

Chapter 7 (1981) I'm Not Smart Enough to Do Math 69

Chapter 8 (1987) Grandpa Dies as I Rebuild.....83

Chapter 9 (1988) Becoming a Wife Again and a Stepmother for the First Time 115

Chapter 10 (1991) Having a Son 121

Chapter 11 (1996) Elvis' Birthday, the Snowstorm of the Century and Absolute Absence of Sleep 127

Chapter 12 (1999) I Cannot Save My Father ..159

Chapter 13 (2004) Going Home to NKU and the Descent into Darkness......................175

Chapter 14 (2010) Moving to Four States in Five Years 195

Chapter 15 (2016) Lessons Learned from Falling out of the Bathtub on the Other Side of the World 257

Chapter 16 (2017) Finally Home 265

Preface

This book will likely surprise many people in my personal circle. Throughout my life, I have presented a brave front to the world. In fact, I remember a former employer describing me as one of the most independent women they had ever met.

I have always been proud of my ability to problem solve through difficult situations, and soldier on. The truth though is that along the way I have felt not only successful, but also terrified at times. The highs in my life have been many. The lows have been heartbreaking, and debilitating. I have fought with myself, with God, and raged against the machine before I learned that what I really needed to do was reach out, and ask for help when needed. Most importantly, I had to learn that sometimes the answer is there is no answer. Some things just are.

This book is rooted in my most honest recollection of the journey I have taken. It is very personal, and I must share that I feel quite vulnerable releasing it. I also have been unable to resist the calling that I have had for quite some time that I need to do just that. It is in the spirit of hoping that this will reach even one person and help them along their pathway that I offer it. I am convinced that I am in a more positive place because others have reached out to me, and I want to now step up and pay it forward.

In the writing of my memoir, the stories do not only belong to me. I well realize that there are intersections here that include family, friends, co-workers and others who have helped to write the story of my life. I have expressed it with the utmost care, honesty and love. The story is painful at times, and I do not take the responsibility of including those details lightly. It would be incomplete without sharing these difficult chapters. Know that I worked diligently to reflect the positive that evolved because of the valleys along the way.

I would be remiss if I did not thank those in my life that have supported my effort to produce, *Circling The Drain*. I am so grateful for my family and friends, who I turn to in every endeavor that I pursue. I am blessed to be called daughter, mother, grandmother, wife, sister, niece, aunt, cousin and friend. God has blessed me with more people in my life than I can name here. Two that I must thank however are my husband, Evan, and my writing coach, Christina Young. The two of you have stood in the trenches with me, patiently encouraged me day by day until I

finally stand at this precipice. Thank you from
the bottom of my heart.

Chapter 1 (1969) Jax, Jumping Rope, and Wetting Your Pants

I am woman, hear me roar in numbers too big to ignore and I know too much to go back and pretend, cause I've heard it all before, and I've been down there on the floor, No one's ever gonna keep me down again~ I Am Woman, Helen Reddy

I actually did fall out of the bathtub on the other side of world in the summer of 2016. It is a true, hilarious, and somewhat terrifying story to share. To understand it fully, though, you need to understand how I came to end up there, and for that, I have to take you all the way back to 1969.

1969 feels simultaneously like such a long time ago and yesterday all at once. I was a young girl, just six years old. The world was a giant, magical place. The days seemed longer, the sun a little brighter, and everything was full of promise. I grew up in a modest neighborhood in Northern Kentucky. I remember thinking that my house was the most beautiful one on the street. Friends were plentiful, and life was good. At the end of that summer, I was preparing to go to first grade, and was more than a little excited about that prospect.

In what would become a yearly tradition, my mother took me to JC Penneys to purchase new shoes. I did not take long to choose what I wanted. The new penny loafers were what I instantly knew I needed to buy. We took them home, after the ride on the coin-operated horse, and my mother found two new pennies to insert into the openings. Everything was set!

School began in the usual flurry of activity. I quickly settled into riding the bus the short distance between my home and my school with my older sister, Karen. I was the only person I knew, except my sister, whose mother worked outside the home. So at the end of the day we also rode the bus home. We let ourselves into the house with our key. At that time, I was a bit unhappy about that situation. I did not understand why my mom was not able to be home when I arrived. She was not too far behind us each day, and came through the door and went into her second shift activities. Namely, getting dinner started, homework checked, laundry going, and all of us ready for the following day. As I grew older, I appreciated her ability to handle so much, so well, more and more. My first step down that road began with a very powerful lesson.

In the early fall of my first grade year, I found myself at recess, sitting with the girls who were given chalk, jump ropes, and jacks to play with. I was growing increasingly bored with those activities and looking across the playground at the boys who were participating in foot races. The winner would ask for a new challenger, and whoever was victorious would challenge the next boy in order to see who was the fastest on the playground. Eventually, I found myself unable to resist the urge to ask to join them. They laughed at me, but agreed.

I was dressed in my new shoes, and a brown, plaid dress with big pockets on the front of it. I got ready to race the current winner, and remember how wonderful it felt to be running across the blacktop. I won that match, and returned to the line to challenge the next boy.

This continued a few times, and I continued to win. I lined up to race the final challenger. I ran as fast as I possibly could, but he was pulling ahead of me. I pushed harder and at the edge of the blacktop found myself unable to stop. I stumbled forward into the muddy grass, eventually falling down. Both of my shoes became stuck in the mud and one of the pockets on my dress was torn. By the time I got myself upright a very unhappy schoolyard monitor with a very serious hair bun was standing over me.

She frowned, and then began to scold me. "Kimberly, look at what you have done! You have spoiled your dress and shoes. Ladies are not supposed to behave this way. You are going to hurt yourself, AND you are going to make the boys feel bad because you beat them!"

I still remember the deep shame that poured over me. I believed every single word that she had said, and found myself wondering how I would ever make things right. I rode the bus home and for once was happy my mother was not there. I took off my dress and shoes and hid them in my closet. I waited and eventually heard the familiar sounds of my mother coming in the front door. As usual, she flew into her evening routine, but she began to notice that I was uncharacteristically sullen. Before long, I found I could not hold everything in any longer. I began to cry, and the whole, awful story spilled out. I will never forget the quiet that fell over my mother and the entire kitchen. She asked me if I knew what a whipstitch was. I shook my head and she took me by the hand to sit down with her as she retrieved my dress and shoes. She placed a thread through a needle, and began to sew my pocket back in place on my dress. I watched in wonder as she explained how easy it was to fix. She then went on to clean the mud off my shoes, and replace the pennies with two new, shiny ones. She then proclaimed that everything was as good as new and went on to the task of dinner.

I was relieved, but still troubled. Things should be back to normal, I remember thinking, but somehow something was off. I went to bed and woke up in the morning feeling the same unsettled way. It was then that my mother surprised me again. This time, she announced that I would not be riding the bus to school, but instead that she was driving me there herself. Up the long drive we went, but instead of dropping me off, she proceeded to park and then got out of the car. She walked straight into the front door with me, and instead of turning right towards my classroom she turned left and walked into the principal's office. Mr. Huber was a kind, gentle man, and seemed surprised to see my mother there. She asked to speak with him and the playground monitor from the day before. I sat in amazement as I watched my mother quietly explain that she expected her daughter to be treated the same as everyone else, whether on the playground or in the classroom. She waited for assurances that I could choose to jump rope or foot race as I liked. She then got up to leave. She paused at the door, and then turned around and looked straight at me. "Have a good day. And remember, if those boys can't keep up with you, that's THEIR problem!"

If was as if a key turned a lock inside of my head at that moment. All of my unsettled feelings transformed to feelings of accomplishment. At the age of six, I realized I had not created an issue because I did something wrong. I created an issue because I did something unexpected. Doing something unexpected does not equate to doing something wrong. It laid a foundation that I was to test again and again.

Fast forward a few years and you will find me in third grade. I loved school, and looked forward to going each day. There was a pressing problem that was becoming increasingly troublesome for me. It was deeply personal, and caused me shame. For several years, the inability to stop wetting my pants became more and more difficult to deal with. If I jumped off the playground monkey bars and both of my feet hit the ground at the same time, there was an accident. Sneezing, laughing, and coughing produced similar results. In addition, for no reason, with no warning, a sudden urge to use the bathroom could not be denied and I would find myself once again in shame, in urine soaked clothes.

The positive about this situation is that it was one of my first, and most powerful lessons in empathy. I remember being in class one sunny day. Our teacher had just allowed us to push our desks into pods of four each. The desks were small, and had chairs that were not attached to them. It was unusual to find our teacher in a grouchy mood, but that particular day she was just that. I remember raising my hand to ask to use the restroom, and she said no, that recess was just a short time away and I should wait until then. I panicked. I felt the all too familiar urge growing and raised my hand again to repeat my request. She was more direct in her denial the second time. I sat there and watched the hands of the clock literally stop as I waited for the recess bell to ring. Inevitably, I lost control, and it was at that point that I saw urine streaming down the legs of the chair forming an ever-widening puddle around my shoes.

My teacher looked up and our eyes met. I was frozen, and had not raised my hand, or said a word, but she immediately sensed that something was wrong. She then stood and announced that everyone was free to go to recess immediately. Amid shouts and cheers, my classmates ran out the door into the spring air. That was when my teacher cautiously walked towards me and saw why I was still sitting down. I remember wishing that I could just die and have my whole body disappear, sort of like when the Wicked Witch of the West disappeared after the bucket of water landed on her. I began to cry. I will never forget the compassion that washed over her face, and her assuring me everything was going to be OK. She said how sorry she was for not allowing me to go the restroom when I asked. Then she cleaned everything up before anyone came back into our room. No one but she and I knew it had even happened.

Looking back, as an adult, I now appreciate that on one of her worst days, she had the compassion and empathy to step out of her own day and into mine to provide help. I went home that day and shared what had happened. I was taken to the doctor because it was now evident that this was not something that was going to go away. It was discovered that I had an issue that required two surgical procedures across the next two years to help me gain control over this most basic function. The problem would resurface throughout my lifetime, and land me in a situation where the people around me set the example for how to treat someone with cruelty, causing great pain. That story will have to wait until I grow up and encounter Valdosta, Georgia.

Chapter 2 (1971) Finding Jesus and Losing Myself

Put your hand in the hand of the man who stilled the water, put your hand in the hand of the man who calmed the sea~Put Your Hand In The Hand, Anne Murray

I have warm, wonderful memories of growing up at Bellevue Baptist Church. It was a community of people that included family and friends, and going there was embedded into the fabric of our family life. It was a safe place for me during my earliest years. As I grew older, it also became a paradox.

There is something so comforting about the sight, sounds, and even the smell of the familiar church sanctuary. The traditions it holds can help to undergird the foundation that you build upon. You begin to understand that there is something much larger than you that is in charge of the universe. No matter what your belief system, no matter how you connect to that place, a commonality extends across all of us. We turn to that power in times both good and bad. I can remember being very happy, and at peace at our small, tight-knit church. Sunday school, vacation bible school, choir, all sewn together with favorite hymns and favorite people each week helped me to grow in my faith.

I would find that faith tested on so many occasions. At the worst points in my life, I often turned from that faith. Sometimes filled with bitterness, and the feeling that God surely had abandoned me when bad things happened. I thought, when I was younger, that if I did what I was told was the right thing to do, then life would fall in line. Resulting in the inevitable promise that would be fulfilled with entering the gates of heaven when I died. In addition, as a young girl, that scenario was played out only after a long, happy, fulfilling life. One that was blessed with a husband, children and prosperity and all that life had to offer. I began to question that philosophy early.

One of my earliest lessons was that I was unique. At that point in my life, and for many, many years afterwards, I looked at that uniqueness as a negative. Something that made me, "other-than" and inevitably, "less-than." I began to question, and question, and question.

When I was about seven, I was standing in the long line at the end of the church service, waiting to get a hug from our pastor, and watch my parents exchange pleasantries. It was our tradition, before heading off to lunch as a family. Sometimes that would mean going for hamburgers, other times it meant going to the deli to take home sandwiches.

That particular Sunday, I had a question that had been bubbling up throughout the entire morning. I had watched as the Pastor delivered the message. He was the clear leader of the service and the church. I had always known that his wife was the piano player, but it was not until that morning that I noticed that all of the leaders were men. Moreover, even though I could not understand or articulate what I was noticing, it was the first memory I have of realizing that the people in power were predominantly men. White men. As my turn approached, I decided to ask the Pastor the question that was on my mind. I spoke up. "So if you are a boy, you can be the PASTOR, but if you are a girl, you can only be the piano player. Right?"

I clearly remember the silence that fell all around me. Anyone who was in earshot stood still, and I became painfully aware that I had somehow really crossed an invisible line. That feeling of being other-than came bounding back to me. I could not figure out what I had done. I only was able to read the unspoken messages that it was not a good thing.

The Pastor looked at me for what felt like a very long time, and then straightened up so he was eye level with my father. He put his left hand on my father's shoulder, and shook his hand at the same time, saying, "Jim, good luck with this one. You have your work cut out for you!"

There was nervous laughter, and we filed out of the church. My father was displeased with me. He felt I had been disrespectful to the Pastor. I struggled with trying to figure out how to reconcile wanting to please my father, but also feeling that I had asked a question that still needed an answer. It was a journey that I began in earnest that day. I continue it to this moment.

Is there a way to find that balance? Being true to yourself, but also be pleasing to those who you love and care about?

That answer is one that I continue to chase, nearly fifty years later. The lesson I have learned is that to truly answer it, I have to take a deep dive into my very soul. To figure out where my moral compass really lies, and how to stay true to it. Before I came to this realization, I went down more than a few rabbit holes.

One of those holes began as I found myself being placed in charge of different events at a very young age. On one hand, it is a compliment to gain the trust of teachers and others who gave me opportunities to explore leadership. On the other hand, it was a conflict on two levels. I had become aware at a young age that girls, and women, were not recognized as leaders in the same way as boys and men. The second conflict came as I tried to carry out duties assigned to me, which at times placed me at odds with my friends and classmates.

At the end of my kindergarten year, Richard Nixon was the President of the United States, and I was chosen to be the co-valedictorian of my class. The teachers pulled out our lunchroom tables and covered them in bright white crepe paper. A small box was placed in front of one, and I walked up onto the surface of one of the tables and gave a speech that I had rehearsed to welcome the guests to graduation. I still remember the shine of my patent leather shoes, and the man who photographed me at the end for my formal picture. Looking back, it was a big responsibility for a five year old. It was also the first time that I experienced that some of my friends were unhappy with me because they were not the one chosen to be standing on that table. It was a mixed bag of emotions for me. I wanted to make my parents and teachers proud, but was also quite nervous. I also was unhappy at the uncomfortable messages I was clearly receiving from a few of my friends.

Later, in second grade, my teacher, who had a big rocking chair in her classroom, would often leave me in, "charge" of the room if she had to step out. One day, she instructed me to write the names of anyone who talked on the board while she was away. One of my best friends was talking and laughing, and after a struggle within myself, I got up from that big rocking chair. I took a piece of chalk, and wrote her name on the board. When the teacher returned, Joyce was reprimanded. And things were never quite the same between us after that.

So the quagmire I found myself falling into became deeper. How was I to determine what was the right thing to do? How would I reconcile doing the thing I thought was right with the price that I found I was paying with friends? I think back to that little girl, and can see now where the conflict began. I had a very strong female role model in my mother. I also was cognizant that there was a basic inequity in the world, even as small as the circles were that I moved in, between the genders. My exposure to friends of color was nearly non-existent. I also wanted to be liked. I had the same universal desire to be accepted as part of the peer group that I found myself in, but again, wanted to please my teachers. I could not know it then, but it was the seed that was eventually going to germinate into my search for my most sacred values. The values that would become my waypoints and serve me in good stead when I was called upon to finally stand up and say, "enough" when forced into untenable situations with spouses, employers, and family and friends. Much later in my life, I would finally draw a line in the sand that would separate me from some of those who I loved the most in the world.

Chapter 3 (1975) Cover Girl and Hiding

Don't look at me. Everyday is so wonderful, then suddenly it's hard to breathe. Now and then I get insecure from all the pain. I'm so ashamed. I am beautiful, no matter what they say. Words can't bring me down. I am beautiful in every single way. Yes words can't bring me down. Oh no. So don't you bring me down today~Beautiful, Christina Aguilera

I well remember when I was totally comfortable in my own skin. With my appearance. Happy to be me, in the body that I was born into. I had a transistor radio that could pick up AM stations, and I spent many, happy hours listening for my favorite songs to come on. The Carpenters, Tom Jones, and The Grass Roots topped that list. On the best days, I would have my radio in the basket of my green bicycle, and would be riding up and down the street in the neighborhood where I spent my first fourteen years.

There is not a defining moment in time, or incident, that marks the change from cycling up and down the street, wind in my hair, singing at the top of my lungs, to the person I began to change into. It came on slowly, but relentlessly.

27

The feeling of being different, or other-than inside, found the perfect partner. The certainty that the outside of me was also different, other-than, and just not as good as anyone else I was able to identify with. I turned to magazines, like Seventeen, and tried every suggestion that was offered in their articles. I can remember washing my hair with mayonnaise, scrubbing my nose to remove blackheads so vigorously I removed the skin and caused a scab, and relentlessly shaved every inch of my legs.

Then I discovered make-up. Cover Girl to be exact. Now that I am older, I marvel at how genius that product line name actually is. All I wanted to do was cover up. Hide every perceived flaw. By the time I arrived at the first day of school in eighth grade, I had not only begun a meticulous routine of applying heavy make-up, I also began to spend copious amounts of time grooming my hair. All I could see when I looked in the mirror were flaws and imperfections. I began to hate every part of myself.

What is more painful, though, is that the routine I slowly became enslaved to was often misinterpreted as vanity. Me running carelessly through money for products that I did not need, and spending hours grooming and staring at myself in the mirror. I was unable to explain the need I felt to make things perfect. To try to be perfect. To get things right, the way I thought everyone around me could. I could not do it, and I continued to retreat into my routine. Endlessly buffing my nails to attain a shine no one could achieve. Laying out clothes each evening, trying desperately to color coordinate everything right down to my underwear. Meticulous is a good word to discuss the routine I had fallen into. I was so sure that if I did not perform all of the new rituals, I should not even leave my house. I simply felt that I could not face the world without going through all of the motions.

My world grew smaller as a result. I literally began to hide from people if I had not had the opportunity to go through my entire regiment. I would not go outside without it. I would not accept invitations to sleep over with my girlfriends at their houses. If I did go, I would eventually feign an illness and return home to the comfort of my own bed and room where I felt the sanctuary that I craved.

Looking back, with time and introspection, I see now that this was the beginning of major self-doubt. The time when I had both the inner doubt, meet the physical doubt about my appearance. Things spiraled downhill for so many years afterwards. How could I ever learn to love and embrace myself?

As I watch the world that we live in today unfold, I am very thankful that I grew up in a world before social media. The non-stop access that everyone has to one another is simply frightening. There is no retreat from the spotlight. An all-out race to stage the perfect appearance and the perfect life. None of it is real, but that is hard to discern when you look at it from a distance. It exacerbates the feeling that one is not living up to some imagined ideal. I watch in wonder as I see people spend copious amounts of time to perfect a selfie to post, and then spend the rest of the meal, or whatever the activity is, not even interacting at all. The picture would suggest that there is a harmonious life that is being lived. The reality is far different in so many instances. When this layer is placed on top of the feeling that many of us have, that somehow we just are not good enough, well, that is a recipe for disaster.

Many years later, I found myself not only teetering on the brink of the very disaster I am describing, but literally falling into the abyss. It was a terrible, dark day when every option seemed to close in front of my eyes. My belief that I could not get it right was worse than it ever had been in my life. Social media pounced on me when I was at my most vulnerable, and the viciousness with which it pounced astonishes me still many years later. I did not reach out to anyone for help in my isolation, because I just truly believed no amount of work, make-up, or assistance could ever make things right again. Thankfully, I was wrong, and more thankfully, there was someone with compassion who was paying attention and literally saved my life. For the rest of that story, we need to wait until 2015.

Chapter 4 (1977) On Fire:
Beverly Hills and Leo

You had a hold on me right from the start. A grip so tight I couldn't tear it apart. My nerves all jumpin' actin' like a fool. Well, your kisses they burn, but my heart stays cool~Fire, The Pointer Sisters

The summer before my high school experience began was one of transformation. Both physically and spiritually, I found myself changing, and questioning everything that had come before. My thoughts about the validity of my church teachings were in constant dialogue in my head. I wrestled with their teachings and the experiences I was beginning to have as a teenager. I found myself trying desperately to individuate from my parents, and yet I was terrified to be on my own. I channeled all of that ugly behavior at my mother. I regret that to this day.

My feelings of being different became even more pronounced as I entered my mid-teenage years.
The summer of 1977 brought with it two events that changed how I saw the world forever.

In May of that year, I found myself fresh out of 8th grade, and at the home of one of my best friends, celebrating our new freedom with the summer completely ahead of us. It was then that we got the news that The Beverly Hills Supper Club was on fire. This was long before instant access to the news, and 24-hour coverage. There were no cell phones, and no internet to access.

The Beverly Hills Supper Club touted itself as, "The Showplace of the Nation." And it truly was. We passed it often, as we drove out Route 27 to visit with my grandparents each weekend. It sat high up on a hill, with a long, winding drive that had one lane up, and one lane down to access the property. At the bottom of the hill was a marquee that listed who was performing that night. It was not unusual to see the elite of Hollywood listed there. Frank Sinatra. Dean Martin. This particular evening, John Davidson was scheduled to perform, and it was to a packed house.

The demand for the show was so great, they brought in extra chairs to fill the room where people were dining, and placed them in the aisles between the tables. The property was a huge, rambling, somewhat disjointed structure. Over the years, it had been remodeled and added onto. It had once before suffered damage through a fire and was rebuilt. There were rumors of mafia activity, and illegal gambling, and VIP access to parts of the club that regular patrons never saw.

I had been to Beverly Hills on several occasions. Sometimes we were treated and went with our parents. Most often, school functions would be held there. In fact, the week before the tragic fire occurred, I, and most of my friends, had been to a track and field end of the year banquet. I still remember the fountains, and the grand staircase, and the mirrors that hung on every wall.

As the fire grew that night in May, 1977, we heard siren after siren after siren in the distance, and first responders raced past us on the street. We waited for the details to unfold. And unfold they did.

When the morning came, we learned that our state had just made history with the worst fire disaster in the history of the country. It would take years for the investigations to be completed. What we did know, was that 169 people had died that night, all dressed up, out on the town, with no idea that they would never see the morning. The governor of the state flew up. There is one terrible photo of him sitting, head in his hands, on a piece of lumber on the ground, the entire structure burned to the ground behind him. There were so many lessons learned that night by all of us.

I came face to face with mortality that morning. Everyone knew someone who was lost in the fire. We all were very aware that only a handful of days separated our last visit there and the night of the tragedy. The bodies were first laid out on the hillside of the property, and later moved to the Fort Thomas Armory, which was where we regularly attended dances and canteens. I never again passed that hillside, or went to the dances without feeling a sense of doom and loss. Our world had been divided somehow into the innocence of the evening before the fire, and the reality of the morning after.

John Davidson had not spoken of this event until recently. It affected his life in such a transformational way; it was almost as if he was from the neighborhood like the rest of us. His musical director died in the fire, and he, along with his associates, spent several days searching through the makeshift morgue that was set up to locate his musical director's body. There are photos that show that he held the door open that he escaped through to help others to safety. It was a horrible night.

We learned a lot about fire codes, and violations, and the price that is paid when making money is placed higher on the list of priorities than human safety. Doors had been chained shut from the outside with padlocks because the owners believed it would cut down on people slipping out without paying their bill. What happened that night was that the lights went out, people found their way to the emergency exits, and instead of escaping, fell victim to the acrid smoke from the burning building and furniture. Many were found stacked on top of one another. The desperation that they must have felt gives me pause to this day.

As the summer progressed, the fire was never far from us, as it was covered each night on the news. People often spoke of the loss of a friend or family member. High school was squarely ahead of me, and my feelings of discomfort and not knowing how to fit in grew. Band camp was to be held in August, a few hours' drive into the middle of Kentucky. I was terrified to go, and have anyone see me without my make up on and without the ability to hide anywhere when the terrible feelings came. I told my mother I thought I would simply not go. She told me it was my decision, which was something I was grateful for. I was also very grateful that I did decide to go, and not rob myself of the experience.

The second transformational event that happened that fateful summer can be summed up in three letters: LEO. It was the summer that I discovered Barry Manilow, as well as KISS. Music would play a powerful role that year and every other year of my life. The intersection of band camp and Leo was almost more than I could take.

I can remember my father thinking the world was ending when Gene Simmons showed up in skintight leather, fully outfitted with make-up to seal the role of The Demon in the rock band, KISS. It was fabulous if I am to be honest. They sang about wanting to rock and roll all night, and party every day. Barry Manilow, on the other hand, seemed to have some particular insight into my soul, crooning about unrequited love and the human connection. Then, just when I least expected it, Leo showed up in my universe.

Leo was a senior. He was tall, gorgeous, outgoing, outspoken, and incredibly talented. He was just one of those people who seemed to be good at anything he tried, and people just gravitated to him naturally. He was the life of every party, and a drummer in the band.

Moreover, before too long, he was paying attention to me, and I was certain I had found my soul mate.

Leo was also African-American. I was not. And it was not well received in 1977, sometimes not even by some of my own family members. Therefore, I went covert with my love affair. Which made it even more tantalizing. The feeling that it was forbidden, and that our love was so great we had nothing to do but to give into it. On the last night of band camp, he kissed me, and I was completely, utterly, helplessly crazy for him.

It is so funny looking back now as an adult, that the few short weeks that I spent, "with" Leo felt like it was much longer than it really was. I spent most of my freshman year strategically positioning myself in the hallways where I thought he might walk by, and gazing at him across the band room like a love struck goof. I was certain that no man would ever fill his shoes again in my lifetime. The time I spent with him was actually very innocent. It was all new to me and I found myself really wondering about the feelings I was having and the teachings I had learned about in church. I did not act on what I really wanted to do, and all these years later can honestly say I am glad for that. He was also very young, and now I understand what happened in a way that I could not possibly comprehend at that time.

Years later, I learned that life had been challenging for Leo. He got sick, and one sad day I learned he had died in another state from his illness. I had not seen him for years, but sat down that day and cried. The memorial service that was held for him at home found us all drawn together into a church that was full to capacity. He had been cremated, and I sat there just dumbfounded that his light was gone, and he now was just in my memory. I remember blogging at the time that Leo represented the best of all of us kids from Newport. I still cannot believe he is gone.

Chapter 5 (1978) The Newport Girl

In a little while from now, if I'm not feeling any less sour, I promise myself to treat myself, and visit a nearby tower. And climbing to the top, will throw myself off, in an effort to make it clear to whoever wants to know what it's like when you're shattered~Alone Again, Gilbert O'Sullivan

The summer after my first year of high school was very traumatic for me. Besides the fact that I had watched Leo graduate, and having no idea if I would ever see him again, my parents made the decision to move to another city. One of the constants in my lifetime was my house on Grand Avenue in Newport. Now, I was faced with the prospect of going up the hill to Fort Thomas. In reality, it was only a few miles away. Nevertheless, for my purposes, it might as well have been in another solar system.

Newport, Kentucky will always be the place I consider home. It has a very storied past that is chronicled in the expose, "Girls, Guns, and Gambling." There was a lot of mafia presence in Newport in the early and mid-1900s and that most northern part of the state made a deal with the devil, so to speak. For years, Northern

Kentucky did not ask for much from the state, and the state was asked to simply look the other way with regard to any illegal activity happening there. When some of the citizens decided to clean up the city, the illegal activity came into a glaring light, and finally they prevailed and literally ran the bad guys out of town. What no one realized, was that the bad guys left and took all of their money with them. For a few decades, my hometown fell into disrepair, and often people hung their heads when admitting they were from Newport. Fort Thomas, on the other hand, was a neighboring city with affluent residents. It was named, "The City of Beautiful Homes." All we knew was that the kids there drove cars that we could never afford, and that we were from the other side of the tracks.

Learning that I was being moved to this foreign land was news I was not happy about. At all. I could not fathom at that age what my parents were thinking. Looking back, I now know that it was a move on their part to get into a better financial position, with a better home, and away from some of the unsavory activity that had begun to creep into our neighborhood. For me, it simply felt like the world was ending.

I was given the choice to either stay at Newport High School, or transfer to Highlands High School. That was a no brainer for me. I was intimidated by the thought of trying to fit in at Highlands High School. I had also come to believe that my academic skills, especially in the area of mathematics, would not allow me to be successful. I chose to stay where I was comfortable, and knew I was among friends. It did not take long for the landscape to change.

I have always thought how ironic it was that people in Newport came to believe that we were rich since we had moved up the hill to Fort Thomas. We were not rich by any stretch of the imagination. Conversely, there was a perception about me in Fort Thomas that was also incorrect.

About six months after moving, I met a boy, a year older than me, on my street. Mike was tall, handsome, and had a car. We began to date, and he introduced me to a few of his friends. One day, after school, I went with him to his best friend's house, along with several other teenagers. David's mother came home from work, and was visibly upset. She called David into the kitchen and pulled the shutters between them and us. It was a futile effort to keep us from hearing their conversation. David kept asking what was wrong. She kept responding that either she or his father had to be home if he had friends over. When he kept protesting that had never been the case she finally yelled, "It is OK for your friends to come over after school. We do not have to be home if it is your friends. But if THAT NEWPORT GIRL is here, then one of us has to be home. You KNOW how those Newport girls act!"

I wanted to disappear. Just fall through the floor, never to return. This had become an all too familiar emotion by that point in my life. David came back into the room, laughing quietly. Mike got up to leave, and as we opened the door, David called out, "See you later Newport girl!"

The name stuck. His friends began to use it. Years later, as a young mother, myself now raising my own children in Fort Thomas, I felt the sting of that nickname again. I was helping at the annual fundraiser for my children's school, and was assigned to help take pictures with Santa Claus. There was a long line of children and parents, and the day was going well, when I heard, "Hey, It's the NEWPORT girl!" David was in line with his own children. We were both grown up, with children of our own, but David still refused to call me by my name.

On the other side of the equation, in Newport, I found myself riding the bus home my sophomore year as I was not quite old enough to drive. I waited on the corner and if I missed the first bus, sometimes stood there for a long while until another one came along. Gone were the days where I could walk home. It was subtle, but the nicknames began to be assigned to me there as well. Students would drive by and yell, "Hey, cake eater!" That was the nickname that the supposedly rich kids in Fort Thomas endured. Meaning that they were so rich all they ever had to eat was cake. I began to realize that I did not fit into either city at that point, and did the only thing I knew how to do to survive. I acted as though it did not bother me. In fact, I could see and feel the chasm between the life I had before the move and the life I had after it widening with each passing day.

At the end of my sophomore year at Newport High School, there were try-outs held for the leadership positions in the marching band. The marching band was my foundation, the place where I felt the most accepted. It was where I felt the most comfortable in my own skin. I made the decision to try out to be the field commander. This was something that was a bit unusual, as that position usually was awarded to a rising senior. There was another sophomore, someone who had been a close friend to me for many years, who also wanted to win that position. Life began to get very ugly for me as the tryouts grew near. To that end, the school board was alerted that I should have to drop out of Newport High School because of my residency in the next town. My parents explored options for me, and ended up going through a legal action that awarded responsibility for me to the parents of another close friend through the school hours each day. So my residency issue was settled. The day arrived, tryouts occurred, and I won. The victory was very short-lived, however.

Two camps began to emerge. One group supported me. The other supported the friend that I had beaten to become the field commander. I well remember going to a football game at the home field of the rival we were playing, and marching down the fifty-yard line to give the opening salute. Some of the people in the other camp were sitting right in the middle of the opposing fans, in Newport jackets and colors, screaming obscenities at me as I tried to hold it together and lead the show. This was the first really impactful lesson where I learned how to be feeling one way, but behave in another as though I was a character watching myself perform on a stage. In one sense, it was a lifesaver. In another, I was at conflict with myself for acting as though it was not happening. I also internalized the deep shame I felt to have complete strangers witness the level of animosity that my own classmates had for me. It was something that continued for the entire football season. I made the decision to not try out again at the end of my junior year of high school, but that made my father very unhappy. So I did try out, and was again placed in the role. There was not a lot about my time there that was positive, as it was so contentious. The message I received at many turns was that I did not belong there, and that I should leave.

One particularly difficult game found me marching into the Fort Thomas high school football field, as we were playing them on their turf. I was in my spot, in front of the band, marching to the cadence of the drums, down the long driveway to the field. Students, and even adults, were lined up on both sides of the driveway, yelling terrible things at us, and even throwing things, like eggs, and mustard. Our new uniforms, that we had worked so hard to raise money to afford, were damaged. Our bus had rocks thrown at it in the parking lot. It was a different day, where it seemed as though that sort of behavior was expected, and accepted. One of the hardest things I remember about that game was seeing neighbors from my street there, jeering at our band as we performed. The Newport Girl was not welcomed there, and neither was my beloved band. It was a lesson for me in how a crowd can galvanize and literally shut a whole group out.

One of the most painful memories for me was a day when I was threatened at school by a supporter in the other camp, who thought my friend should have been named field commander. This was well into the second half of the school year, in the middle of the basketball season. As that Friday unfolded, I was told throughout the day that Sue was going to wait for me after school and beat me up. I went to the principal, who told me that there was nothing he could do until something happened. After school, I waited in the band room, staring out the window at the bus stop I knew I had to go to in order to go home. I intentionally let the first bus pass hoping that Sue would be headed home herself and everything would blow over. Two of my friends were with me in the band room, and when we finally decided to head outside, Sue appeared near the sidewalk with a few of her supporters and the taunts and name-calling began. I tried to walk past them, but as I did, I felt the blows of her fists on the back of my neck and head. One of my friends jumped in and began to hit her back. It got fairly violent, but ended just as quickly. People began to disperse, and I went to the bus stop and stood there numb. I felt knots begin to raise on my scalp, mostly behind my ears. I went home and to my bedroom, and tried to deal with the emotions I was feeling.

There was a basketball game that night, and I
had a responsibility to go to school and lead the
pep band, beginning with directing the National
Anthem at the beginning of the game. My
parents were at all of my events, and this game
was no exception. I made the decision to not
share with them what had happened, but
instead tried to get ready and go about the night
as though nothing had happened. I have one
vivid memory of fixing my hair, and trying to
wear a headband I had bought that I thought
was pretty. It was metal, and hit the knots on
my scalp in such a way as to prevent me from
putting it on. I arrived at school, and years
before the internet and social media, saw just
how powerful communication spreads,
especially news as juicy as this. The gymnasium
was overflowing. It seemed everyone was
there, many people pointing and whispering. I
walked out to the middle of the basketball court
and began to direct the National Anthem, and
made it through most of the game leading songs
like, "25 or 6 to 4" and "Smoke on the Water".
My mother noticed something was amiss. I
turned to her and told her what had happened
earlier that day. She and my father walked me
out to my car, and the enormity of the violation
I felt began to settle in and manifest itself. My
parents eventually took action in the court
system to ensure my safety, but it did not stop

events such as me leaving play practice one evening only to find my 1977 silver Volkswagen Super beetle vandalized. The spark plugs had been tampered with, and the windows had been covered in a thick layer of soap.

I made the decision to stay in school in Newport. It is one of my best qualities, the ability to stand up and fight for justice, and see things through to the end. It is also one of my worst qualities, when it tips over into the place where I continue to soldier on even when it is to my detriment. I have learned how to take a step back as I have grown older, and figure out when that tipping is occurring and recalibrate.

I would be remiss not to share that I had many acts of kindness shown to me during those difficult years. Teachers who helped me learn, grow, and mature. My parents were always a source of support even when I acted out in ugly ways with them, because it was the safest place I knew to go to let the demons loose. I had wonderful experiences, like the trip the band took to Washington, DC, after spending months selling M&Ms and metric rulers to fund raise our expenses to accept an invitation to the Cherry Blossom Festival Parade. I had the opportunity to experience the monuments with my friends, and parents who went as chaperones, and even walked out onto the tarmac at the Tomb of the

Unknown Soldier to lay a wreath as a gift from our group. I have returned there repeatedly over my lifetime, and never have gone to Arlington where I did not marvel at the fact that at one point in my life I was blessed to cross that rope.

What I was learning at this stage in my life is that there are moments of great triumph, and moments of deep sorrow. For all of us. Moreover, that the most important thing is to just keep moving forward. I would stumble many times before I fully began to trust this lesson.

Chapter 6 (1980) Waiting for a Girl Like You and Grilled Cheese Sandwiches

So long. I've been looking too hard, I've been waiting too long. Sometimes I don't know what I will find. I only know it's a matter of time. When you love someone...when you love someone. It feels so right, so warm and true, I need to know if you feel it too. Maybe I'm wrong. Won't you tell me if I'm coming on too strong? This heart of mine has been hurt before. This time I want to be sure.~Waiting For A Girl Like You, Foreigner

One of the gifts that came to me from my involvement in the band was my deep friendships with many of the members there. One of them was with a drummer, named Gary. I had known Gary all of my life, it seemed. He was a year older than me, so from the time I was in first grade I knew who he was, and our paths crossed often as we grew up. We were involved in many of the same activities, and our love of music, and the band was one that brought us together in a very meaningful way.

In the spring of my junior year, Gary ventured out, and asked me to go to the prom. I was in a place at that time where I had decided to not do anything at school that was not absolutely necessary because of the bullying that I was experiencing. So I turned him down. I almost immediately regretted it, as he went on to ask another friend who said yes. So I figured that was that.

In those days, the prom was a weekend event. The dance happened on a Friday night, and then there were picnics, and a day at the local amusement park that followed the Saturday and Sunday afterwards. I was home on Saturday evening when Gary called to say that his date had told him she was going to the amusement park with someone else and he wanted to know if I would go with him the next day. I said yes, and we were inseparable from that moment forward.

Gary was not really in the popular group of students outside of band. He wore thick glasses, and was introverted, and we just connected in a way that I thought was so meaningful. He seemed to understand the feelings I had of feeling other-than. He was fun to be with, and he was endlessly devoted to me. He also was graduating. I can remember playing the pomp and circumstance as he filed in with his classmates to graduate that spring. I was unsure what I would do at school without him, as he had become such a support in my life.

We had a wonderful summer, then I entered my senior year, and he went to college on a campus that was very near Newport. Northern Kentucky University was just a few miles away, and he was able to go there and still live at home. In the fall of my senior year of high school, he proposed. I was ecstatic. My mother was less so. She tried to explain to me that there was so much life to be lived, so much change that was in front of us, and that we really were far too young to be considering marriage. I chose to ignore all of that advice, and charged ahead with our plans.

In the backdrop of my life during this period, Foreigner seemed to endlessly be on the radio, singing their hit song, "Waiting For A Girl Like You."

Looking back, I now know that the lesson I learned from this was to take a step back. That mistakes are not usually made because we do not act quickly enough. Oftentimes they are made when you do not widen your blinders and look to the left and the right and figure out the whole picture.

Once it was clear to my parents that this was my choice, they both supported our decision. We planned the wedding for December of 1982. I spent hours figuring out how to be the perfect Christmas bride. After graduating high school in 1981, I went to Northern Kentucky University for one academic year, but quit to take a job working full time on campus. At the time, I was making $4.35 an hour, and thought I had the world all figured out. My fears of being academically weak were fully formed in my mind, and I thought this was the perfect pathway for me. Our wedding happened, and we planned what we thought was the most romantic honeymoon...a trip to the amusement park that brought us together two years earlier on that prom weekend. It was now completely outfitted as a Christmas wonderland and I could not imagine anything better. I was 19 years old.

As that next year began to unfold, I began to hear a drum beat in my head that was calling me back to school. This drumbeat would continue throughout most of my next 30 years. I began to explore programs at NKU, and settled on a two-year cohort offering that would train me to become an X-Ray Technologist. I applied, and was accepted. I began this intensive course of study in the summer of 1983. I also left my position at the college and accepted an evening role in the library. It was busy, but very rewarding.

Gary began to experience his own challenges in school. He left, and began a series of jobs, eventually landing a role at a Long John Silver's restaurant, in line to learn how to manage the store. This period of my life is one that I consider quiet, and what I naively believed was on track. As I got close to the end of my program, we decided we would like to try to conceive our first child. I found myself pregnant just six short weeks later.

I can remember the dizzying feelings of watching that home pregnancy test turn positive. I was so excited, and terrified all at the same time. We were living in a two-room apartment, and had no idea what we were doing. Nevertheless, we forged ahead. Jessica was born three months after I graduated. By that time, we were in a much larger apartment, settled, and Gary had been named manager of his store. Life appeared to be perfect.

I took a position as a third shift technologist at a local hospital working every other weekend. We began to look for our first home. We eventually did succeed in getting financed to purchase a small house. We also had made the decision to try to conceive another child. This was not welcome news to my doctor, because I had such complications following Jessica's birth. Those complications landed me in the hospital when she was six weeks old, for ten days. They finally discovered I had gallbladder disease, which had caused me to be so sick throughout my pregnancy with her. I had major surgery to remove my gallbladder and the doctors advised against another pregnancy for a few years. Did I listen? Of course not! I had this.

We were very happy to learn that I was pregnant again. The summer right before Jessica's first birthday found us in a major transitional phase that I thought was extraordinarily positive. We had closed on a new home and we shared our intention to vacate our apartment. Gary was doing well at work. We had a big party for Jessica's first birthday, and began to pack the following morning. That was the day the phone call came that changed my life forever.

I had become accustomed to phone calls from Gary's work when he was home. He had several teenagers working shifts after school and into the evenings and it seemed there were always questions that needed to be answered. On that particular afternoon, I answered the phone, and realized I did not know who was on the other end. The giggling girl identified herself as one of

Valerie's friends, who worked at the restaurant. She told me that she thought I should know that Gary was in love with Valerie. That all of the girls at the store wanted to be with him, but that Valerie had won.

I still remember the clothes I was wearing when that call came in. I remember the phone was hanging on the wall, and was a soft, baby blue color. The sunlight was coming through the window, and the pattern on the floor of the kitchen was navy blue and crème. I was making grilled cheese sandwiches, boxes were everywhere, and Jessica was toddling around the apartment. I turned to Gary and said, "This is getting out of hand. You need to tell these girls to stop prank calls to our home."

Something extraordinary happened. Gary literally shape shifted in front of me. That is to say, he became a stranger to me in an instant. Less than that. He seemed to stand differently, his eyes were not the ones I was familiar with, and he was cruel. He looked straight into my eyes, and said, "It's true. I've been trying to figure out how to tell you."

Everything that I thought I knew, all the lessons I thought I had learned, my entire foundation, cracked to the very core at that moment. If I could not count on Gary being the person I believed him to be, what could I count on?

The world appeared to shift into high gear at that point. Meaning everything seemed to be moving forward faster. It was the first time in my adult life that I felt totally helpless to chart my own course. I felt sad. I felt angry. I felt alienated. I felt like a loser. I simply could not understand what was happening because it fell outside every parameter I had ever set up to keep my life on track.

I remember looking around at our apartment, mostly packed up and ready to move to our new, first house, and wondered what choices I had. I went down for a short period of time, thinking that I did not have any. I began to realize the level of betrayal that had happened to me. As the details began to surface, I began to understand that Gary had not only gotten involved with a teenager. He had worked with her to stage elaborate scenarios that would enable him to bring her back to our apartment, to the very bed I shared with him.

As it turned out, I learned that I was working hard to put Jessica to bed before leaving on alternating Fridays and Saturdays to go to work at midnight, only to have Gary pick her up and deliver her to his parents' home shortly after I departed. I would return in the morning, delighted to find a note from him that said, in effect, that he had taken Jessica to his parents' home early that morning before work so I could rest. How much he loved me. I would return to that very bed for a few hours and then go pick Jessica up, saying how thoughtful Gary was to his parents, both of whom never shared that she had spent the whole night. Finally, the whole, ugly truth spilled out. At that point, I was told that a man should never have to, "babysit" his child, so they thought it was OK to keep her.

I threatened Gary. I cajoled. I cried. I tried to pretend that the world that I knew could somehow come back. I knew at a deep level that it never would. I moved to our new house with Gary, because I could not figure out what else to do. There was a definite shift in power within our relationship. We had gone from friends and lovers, and what I thought was soulmates to adversaries. I simply could not see a way out. Moreover, the truth was, I did not want one. I wanted things to go back to what I thought they were before, even though I had discovered that it was all predicated on a lie.

One day after moving into our new house, another event occurred that would change the course of my life again. I am not sure, to this day, what gave me the courage to move in a different direction. Maybe it was the fact that I am my mother's daughter. Maybe it was because enough was enough. I will forever be grateful for finding my voice, and making a decision that would change my life, and the lives of my daughters, one only one year of age, and the other still unborn.

Gary had fallen asleep, and left his wallet on our bedroom nightstand. I remember that the wallet looked unusual in size and shape. Swollen. I did something I had never done before. I invaded his personal space, and took the wallet into the bathroom, to look at the contents inside.

I was stunned to find letter after letter written by Valerie. They were folded into small triangles, the way we used to do in high school, so we could toss them across the classroom to one another without the teacher noticing what was happening. They were dated, and had long, rambling expressions of love. More disturbing to me, recounts of Valerie either seeing me at the restaurant, or what she and I had talked about when she called our home. There were detailed instructions about ways to schedule interludes. Valerie would explain who she would tell her parents she was spending the night with, and where Gary should pick her up to bring her back to my bedroom. There were so many of them, it made my stomach sick. My hands were shaking as I read letter after letter. I decided to keep them. I left the bathroom, folded up blank sheets of paper into similar triangles, and placed those back into Gary's wallet. I put the real letters into the giant Pampers diaper box in the closet, hoping I would be able to keep them. I then slipped into bed beside Gary, and spent the next hours sleepless, waiting for him to awaken and go to work. The alarm went off, and I feigned sleep with all of my might.

Gary showered, and got ready to depart for work. He picked his wallet up, and for an interminable minute, looked at it. He did not open it, simply turned it over in his hands a few times. He then slipped it into his back pocket and left. With shaking hands, I called my mother at work. I told her what I had learned and that I was ready to leave. I prepared myself for what I believed would be her telling me that she had tried to warn me about this very thing years before. That never happened. She simply said, "I will be there to help you in about half an hour."

My mother showed up. My father did as well. We took my clothes, Jessica's clothes, her crib, and literally walked out the front door. I would return to that house one other time to gather a few other belongings. Gary's parents were there, and they were just furious that I was actually going to move forward with divorce proceedings. I remember that Gary's father was the angriest. He was quite old fashioned, and more than once said that I should stay and, "fight for my man." Actually suggesting that I go challenge Valerie to win him back. He continued to tell my parents, especially my mother, that if they would stop interfering, and helping me, I would need to stay. He then turned and looked at my mother and said, "She better never forget who the father of those children are. She better remember her responsibilities to Gary that way." I was stunned to hear my mother reply, "Kim isn't the problem here. She isn't the one who can't seem to keep her pants zipped." Jim was so angry he actually made a fist, and took a swing at my mother, who was standing against the living room wall. He smashed his fist into the drywall just next to her face. She never moved an inch. I once again was astounded at the way in which she handled a situation that should have intimidated her. If she told me once, she told me hundreds of times that the world was geared to prefer men and boys. She was determined that her daughters would be given equal opportunity and consideration no matter what the cost.

I moved home to my parent's house that fall. I can remember laying in the same bedroom where I had spent my teenage years, and looking at the ceiling, tears rolling into my ears, and thinking this could not be my life. I felt like I had taken a turn somehow, and gone backward in time. Only I had a one-year-old daughter in a crib in the next room, and another baby on the way just six months later so clearly I was not in the same place. My mother kept telling me that I would survive. That with the passage of time I would look back and even be glad that I had gotten out. I was not so sure.

As Christmas crept closer, I began to regroup. I applied for, and won, a full time position at the hospital working second shift. I began to plan to find a way to move into my own place. I felt so strongly that I needed to get me, and Jessica, as well as the baby I had decided I would name Sara, into a place that was clearly ours. I would stand up for my daughters the way my mother had always stood up for me.

I began to quietly look for apartments. I knew my father would not be happy to learn that I was planning on moving out and tackling everything in my own place. I counted on my mother to understand. Until I was able to secure a place, I decided I would wait to share my plans.

On the phone, everyone I called was excited to schedule a visit to the places that they had available to rent. When I showed up for the appointment, holding Jessica on my hip, and visibly pregnant with another child, the tone changed. I was invariably asked where my husband was. When I shared that I was going through a divorce, things went very negative. One person told me it would be a waste of time for me to see the apartment. Another one told me she had just remembered that the apartment was actually already rented. I did not know how to handle the discrimination, and I felt shame at the situation in which I found myself. I had to stop myself from actually explaining to total strangers that this had happened to me, and I needed help.

Things changed when I went to an apartment that was at the upper most limit of my budget. It was in Fort Thomas. I had originally thought I should not even explore it, because it was more than I truly could afford, and had more bells and whistles than I actually had ever had before. There was an attached garage! It was in the same town as my family, and if I was still there when the girls started school, it was in the right school district! It had two floors, two bedrooms, and a washer/dryer included. I showed up, certain that it could never work out. The lesson I learned from this interaction was how powerful empathy and compassion from a total stranger can be.

I toured the apartment with the resident/manager, a woman several decades older than I was. Jessica was with me, and immediately seemed at home in the apartment. Actually, it was a townhouse. We were considering living large! I knew that the rent was $750 a month. My car payment was $250 a month. I was clearing not much more than $2,000 a month after all the deductions from my check. The deposit required was first and last month's rent, which I definitely did not have.

I made small talk, and delayed leaving the place I knew I could not secure. The manager looked at me and said, "If you want the townhouse, I could waive the last month's rent, and arrange for payments for the rest of the deposit if that would help you. You could pay them off and take the unit at the first of the year, and make the first rent payment at the end of that month. Would that help you?"

Stunned, I just whispered, "Why?"

She replied, "I've been in your situation. I see what you are going through. I just want to help."

This was 1986. The stranger before me had just shared something intimate about her past that connected her to me which changed the course of my life. I signed the lease agreement, and went back to share with my parents what I was about to do.

My father was predictably worried and did not want me to leave. My mother was worried as well, but understood why I needed to go. In the end, my family, including my sisters, came together to move me to my new home during the New Year's Eve holiday. I was settled, was scared, felt empowered, and every emotion in between.

Several weeks passed, and then Gary showed back up. On his knees. Begging for another chance. My mother told me not to believe it. I did. She was right, of course. For that lesson, we have to get to 1987.

Chapter 7 (1981) I'm Not Smart Enough to Do Math

I could while away the hours, conferrin' with the flowers, consulting with the rain. And my head I'd be scratchin' while my thoughts are busy hatchin' if I only had a brain~If I Only Had A Brain, E. Harburg

One of the biggest hurdles I ever had to get over was a giant belief system that I internalized, and allowed to cripple me for years. Somewhere along the pathway, in the tumultuous middle school years of my life, I decided I was not smart enough to do math.

I cannot remember making a deliberate decision to feel that way. I cannot even point to one event that would herald the arrival of that falsely held belief. Instead, it was more like an insidious slide into a dark space that I hardly knew was happening. Years later, looking back, I can remember being a younger version of myself, and feeling confident that I could do anything I tackled in school. The self-doubt, and frankly self-loathing that began to take hold as I headed towards my teenaged years are all mixed up with the new programming I was hard wiring into my psyche. Math began to seem like a giant mystery to me, one that most of my friends knew the secret language so they could speak it. I could not.

What I now know is that I internalized a thousand messages that I received. Math is not my strong suite, but I can certainly learn it if it is taught to me in a manner that I can receive it. I also know that I am not alone in this phenomenon, and that others struggle just as much with math and every other subject under the sun.

The worst slide that I took, and the foundation that I laid which took me off track for twenty years occurred when I was a freshman in high school. I had a very bad teacher, and he literally did not do anything by way of instructing our class. The class was a sort of rowdy study hall, and all of our assignments were simply chalked on the board for us to independently complete. So each day we would arrive, and he would have a certain number of pages assigned for us to complete and turn in. The catch? He would allow us to work in groups, the noise level was very high, and the answers to all of the problems were literally in the back of our book. So instead of learning Algebra, which I was too embarrassed to admit looked literally like a different language to me, I punted. We just turned in our papers each day after working together with someone double-checking to be sure our answers matched the ones in the text. The tests were laughable. At the end of each chapter's, "work" we were required to then take the test, which we quickly learned were problems lifted from the text. We were allowed to use our books to access the answers. Everyone passed the class that year, but not all of us learned.

At the beginning of my sophomore year, I found myself in Algebra II. With a very different, stern teacher. I quickly fell behind, and before long was failing the class. A parent/teacher conference was called and my teacher told my parents that I was not Algebra II material. That I needed to be transferred to a less rigorous track and graduate with a diploma that excluded the advanced math classes. I was deeply ashamed, and believed every word he said. My parents did as well, and I was transferred out of that class, and never regained equal footing again until my mid-thirties.

When I arrived at college in 1981, I took the prerequisite general studies classes, and found that I really enjoyed history, and English, but the ugly math monster reared its head once again. I was fully focused on getting married to Gary at this point in time. After spending one academic year as a full time student I decided my time would be best spent by pursuing a full time job, versus continuing on a pathway I was certain I could never walk. Luckily, divine intervention occurred, and the job I found was full time secretarial work at the university. It kept me immersed in the world of academia, and I began to see friends move past me as they progressed on their academic journeys. The faculty that I interacted with also encouraged me to reconsider going back to school. And the drumbeat in my head was calling me to do the same.

I quietly began to consider their advice. I went to the Registrar's office and requested the current paper catalogue of programs. At that time, the Associate Degrees were listed in the back. I never, ever considered a Bachelor's program of study. The reason? They required upper level math credits!

One of the programs that interested me was nursing. I quickly dismissed that idea, as I knew that nurses had to learn how to dispense dosages of medication. Which invariably meant learning more math! The Radiologic Technology program of study caught my attention. As I explored it, I found that it was learning how to take X-Rays, and work in that allied health profession. I remember thinking that I had seen that job in shows on TV. And thinking that they seemed happy, got to wear cute uniforms, and all of the patients appeared to be cheerful. I decided to apply and see if I could get accepted into the cohort for 1983.

The application process involved going for a personal interview to meet with the Chair of the department. Several long weeks passed, and I finally received a letter notifying me that I had been accepted. I was really excited about the prospect of going back to school, and realized that meant I had to resign from my position since the hours would interfere with my class and clinical hours. Divine intervention happened, and a half-time job was posted to work as the Night Supervisor in the Steely Library. It worked with my schedule, and even offered benefits. I applied, and was thrilled to be offered the job. I began the cohort program the following July, shortly after my 20th birthday. Life seemed to be in order.

That summer session consisted of getting acclimated to the program and the responsibilities associated with working in the healthcare setting with patients. Things were going really well, and I was encouraged.

And then the monster appeared. The very first week of the fall semester. And it brought along its' cousin just for fun.

My first day of my clinical rotation, I was up with the chickens. I was so excited to be in my new, white uniform, white shoes, and looking so official. I remember staring at myself in the long mirror on the back of the bathroom door, and had the realization that this was a very big day. That it was transformational in my journey.

Monster number one: I arrived at the hospital, and discovered that we would all be placed in a room for two weeks at a time, to learn the many different examinations that occurred in medical imaging. Patients are sick, scared, and not very happy to be in the hospital. Monster number two? Medical imaging isn't just about taking X-Rays of broken bones. There are myriad exams that happen that involve imaging all of the systems of the body. My first day of clinical I was assigned to the Barium Enema room. Yup. The Barium Enema room!

My confidence waivered. I then learned what happens when a patient is unable to hold the barium that is placed into the large colon. On the walk to the bathroom, my first patient lost it, and as it splashed to the floor, and all over my new shoes, I began to think I made a mistake. I found myself grateful that the clinical days were separated by classroom days, so once I made it home, I was able to have a break. The relief was short-lived.

I arrived the next day to campus and went to, Introductory Physics of Radiation. I hadn't quite connected the fact that if this class involved Physics, there would likely be math involved. I slowly realized that I was not going to have to learn dosages of medication, but how to calculate dosages of radiation. And this was the first class to introduce that concept.

Professor Hawkins entered the classroom, and we all did a double take. He had long, curly hair, a long, curly beard complete with mustache, and big glasses. The impression he left was that his eyes and nose were the only things you could actually see on his face. As the semester went on, and our familiarity with him grew, he was given the nickname, Animal, because someone once correctly pointed out he resembled that character on Sesame Street.

He began to review with the class to see where everyone's skill set was. He would write an equation on the board, and then solve it, and ask if everyone understood what he had just demonstrated. Heads would nod eagerly that they did. I finally did what all first generation college students do. From the last seat in the back of the room, I tentatively raised my hand.

And confessed I did not understand what he was doing. He explained it a second time and asked if I understood it then.

I admitted a second time that I did not understand it at all. He then explained it a third time, and turned to look at me. At that point, I said, that yes, actually it did all make sense then, and to go on. I spent the rest of the class making plans to go to drop/add and withdraw from the program, and see if I could sell my books back and get a refund.

Then something remarkable happened. And taught me the lesson of the impact of an engaged teacher.

Professor Hawkins was ready to dismiss the class, but before he did, he pointed to me, and asked if I would mind to stay for a few minutes after class. I was mortified, and thought maybe he was going to tell me that I wasn't Physics material. I was reliving the humiliation of my sophomore year in high school when I had been advised to leave Algebra II.

He walked back when everyone else was gone and quietly said, "You still didn't understand it, did you?"

I began to talk so quickly that my words were falling over top of one another. I began to explain to him that it was not him, it was definitely me, and that I simply could not do math. I was apologizing and trying to figure out the fastest way to get out of the classroom and to the bookstore so I could sell my books back. The fastest way back to my comfort zone.

He waited until I stopped for a breath, and then took a pen, and a piece of paper, and explained it again, using another approach. He looked at me, and said, "What about now?"

It was as if someone had turned a key and unlocked a deep place inside of my brain. I literally felt it click. I looked at the page, and it was as dramatic as when the color comes on when Dorothy opens the door of her house once it had flown and fallen into Oz.

I understood. He invited me to come in a few minutes early the next class, where he took the time to teach me the lesson, and then I sat and listened to it again with my classmates. I ended up with a low B for my final grade, but I have never been so proud of a grade either before or since.

Another teacher, Andrea, taught me this lesson further. At one point, she assigned our class the project of writing a research paper. I did it. I turned it in, and was surprised when she called me to her office. She was frustrated with me, and I had no idea why. In exasperation she told me that if she had to give me a failing grade on the research paper, it would jeopardize my place in the cohort. She was angry. She kept saying that she could not understand why I had not taken the assignment seriously. How could I have used the textbooks that we had for our classwork as references? I sat wide-eyed, in total confusion. She finally said, "What is the DEFINITION of a research paper?"

I replied in a voice, barely above a whisper, "I don't know."

She sat back. I could see her trying to understand what was happening. I had not tried to cheat. I honestly thought I had completed what was assigned. She then told me she would allow me to turn in another version of the research paper, and spent the next hour teaching me what a research paper actually was.

Ironically, those lessons did not teach me to aspire to reach beyond the Associates degree. For that, I would need another dedicated teacher from my program to keep challenging and stretching me.

My teacher, Kay, would enter my life and spend hours helping me to get out of my own way and matriculate towards graduation. I spent a lot of energy explaining to her how I was not able to do work as well as my classmates, particularly in math. After the first twelve months in my program, working an exhausting schedule of classes, clinical hours, and my job, I made a bad decision. I decided I would drop out of my program at the halfway mark, and take another full time position on campus. I could not envision being able to do it for twelve more months. I fancied myself quite busy taking care of the two-room apartment that Gary and I shared. I told a friend in my class about my plan, and then set out to go to the Human Resources department to officially apply for the job I knew was open.

My friend told Kay. Kay dropped what she was doing, and came to find me. I will never quite forget how upset she was, and how upset I got, when she caught me in the lower level of the administration building. I was standing in front of the mailroom window when she walked up. She asked me what in the world I was thinking. She told me how short twelve additional months were in the overall scheme of things. She challenged me, and said I would not be able to earn a living wage without a degree if I ended up divorced and on my own. I was so offended! Of course, as it turned out, she was completely right. She then literally walked me right back to class. By the time the next twelve months ended, I was pregnant with Jessica, and standing at our official pinning ceremony. Kay called each student forward, and said something unique about each of us. As she pinned my collar with my new credential, she looked at the audience, and said, "I got this one through kicking and screaming."

She was completely accurate.

I returned to visit with Kay after my second daughter was born, and I was officially divorced and on my own, with two children under the age of two. We sat in the cafeteria of the university, and she asked how I was doing. Sara was sitting in a pumpkin seat on top of the table. Jessica was in a high chair between us. I started to cry, and told her I was divorced. She was empathetic, but did not spend much time letting me wallow in my sad story. I asked her what she thought I should do next. I was stunned by her answer.

She began to explain that the department was going to offer a Bachelor's degree in Radiologic Technology. She thought I should go back to school, and work on that milestone. I replied, that it would be too hard, and I was sure I could not do math well enough to be successful.

She said, "Aren't you tired of telling me that story?"

I replied, "It's too much to do. I wouldn't know how to start."

She then slid her spoon across the table and said, "You know how you eat an elephant, don't you? One bite at a time."

I picked that spoon up and dropped it into my diaper bag. I would carry it for the next twenty years. I invited her to Jessica's wedding, wrapped it up, and gave it back to her. Along with a note about the very different place my children and I would both be in if we had taken another route, and she had not convinced me to continue with my academic journey.

The year she gave me the spoon was 1987. I did not cross the stage and receive my Bachelor's degree until 1994. I would remarry, become a stepmother, and have a third child by that date. If I ever was out more than one semester during that time, I would inevitably hear from Kay. The lesson she taught me was that no matter how big the mountain looks, you would eventually reach the summit if you just keep going.

Ten years after I returned the spoon to Kay, I was talking with her about wrestling with my decision to write, and release my memoir. I was not sure I could really do it. It might be too hard.

Shortly after, I saw her. She handed me a gift. I do not know why I thought of it, but I said, "That better not be that spoon showing back up again!"

It was.

This time, it was mounted in a shadow box frame, and had a cute little elephant pendant mounted next to it. The note said, "The older I get the more sure I am...There are ALWAYS more elephants so just in case..."

Sometimes Kay will say I should stop introducing her as my teacher since we now are friends, that in reality are more like family. I have to respectfully disagree. That frame now hangs in my living room, with its' patient message. Just keep going.

Chapter 8 (1987) Grandpa Dies as I Rebuild

I've seen fire and I've seen rain. I've seen sunny days that I thought would never end. I've seen lonely times when I could not find a friend. But I always thought that I'd see you again~Fire And Rain, James Taylor

The advent of 1987 brought many changes to my life. I had settled into a new, full-time position as an X-Ray technologist, working second shifts throughout the week. I had successfully gotten into my new townhouse, and was even beginning to feel a little bit at home. Jessica was doing well in her new bedroom, and I began to earnestly prepare for the arrival of my second daughter. Things seemed to be headed towards the ending my mother had promised me for months. Towards resolution, and even peace.

I retained an attorney and learned that in the state of Kentucky you are not allowed to get a divorce if you are pregnant. I was not happy about that fact, but I was compelled to follow the law. The stress of that time had made the pregnancy quite difficult. Month after month, I went to my doctor to learn I was not gaining the weight I needed. I assured him I was doing the best that I could to manage everything, and take care of myself, Jessica, and my unborn daughter. Just about six weeks before the birth, life threw me another curve.

Gary's return to my life began in subtle ways. A message left on my answering machine. Flowers sent to my work. Then he showed up in my doorway. He was remorseful, and was the person I had known for nearly all of my life again. He told me he had made the biggest mistake anyone could make, and that he knew it. That he was miserable being apart from Jessica and he wanted to come home and rebuild. He wanted to move into the future together and be part of our new daughter's life when she was born.

My mother cautioned me against it. My reaction was to get angry at her and anyone else who did not readily accept my decision to reunite with him. At one point, my doctor said he was not sure he could be civil to Gary if he showed up with me at appointments or at the birth. I dug my heels in, and defended my husband. I told everyone who would listen that anyone could make a terrible mistake. I interceded on his behalf for forgiveness. I told myself I was lucky to have the chance to bring our family back together.

My mother asked me a very reasonable question. "Why would you let him back into your life after you have worked so hard to get away from him and build a new world for yourself and your children?"

Looking back, it is hard to explain even to this day. I did not want to be divorced. I wanted to have a family that I thought was whole. I also have always been a fixer, and a rescuer, so it all played together beautifully to create the next gigantic hurdle.

About six weeks before the birth of our second daughter, Gary and I were doing a quiet dance that we tried to pretend meant we were going to be alright again. I tried, for the sake of my children, and my own sanity, to do all I could to make it through to what I believed would be a new day. That was when the second shoe dropped with regard to our future. Another phone call came. This time the news was even worse.

"Hi! I'm one of Valerie's friends. We thought you should know that she is pregnant!"

Laughter ensued and the line went dead. I drove out to the restaurant, Jessica in tow, and walked in to confront Gary head-on. It was divine intervention that Valerie was not working that night. Gary dropped his eyes, and then his head in shame and sat down in a booth, and told me that it was true. He cried, and pled, and at the end of it all I just became so upset, I discovered what the phrase, "being beside yourself" truly meant. It was such an extraordinary experience, because I literally have no memory of leaving the restaurant. My next cohesive thought about that night found me sitting outside of my parents' house, in my car, crying. Jessica was strapped into her seat and was crying as well. My parents were knocking on the car window. They helped me out of the car, and into the house, and I told them the whole terrible truth. I can remember my father placing a call into the service for my doctor because I was so upset I was not breathing well. I did manage to calm down, gathered myself together enough to take Jessica back to our little townhouse and put her to bed, and laid down myself.

It was a long, long night. I stared at the ceiling, got up and paced the floor, and tried again to understand how I had arrived at that moment in time. Morning arrived, and I went through the motions with Jessica until it was time to head into work. Work was a welcome distraction. Gary continued to call and plead to reconcile. I met him several days later, and agreed that even with this latest turn of events I would be willing to put our family back together. We moved forward and finally the day arrived for Sara to enter the world.

It was a beautiful, sunny, unseasonably warm day when she arrived. It was a Wednesday, and I can remember my doctor saying, "Man, what a gorgeous day to have a baby!" He was quite aloof to Gary, barely acknowledging that he was even in the room. My mother was there and provided the support I needed, but I also felt stressed to make small talk to get her and Gary to interact. Gary had agreed to go to counseling as a concession for coming home, and he had an appointment that very day. We were told that I was a long way from the delivery, so late morning found Gary leaving for an hour to keep his appointment with the counselor.

He was not gone long, when things began to move very fast for me. This predates any sort of cell phone technology, so I had no way to reach him. Sara was born, and my mother was the one who was at my side, and cut the umbilical cord. Gary came shortly afterwards, and was unhappy that he had missed it. I felt the uneasiness return as he and mom were so awkward around one another.

Sara was small, and I had gained less than ten pounds throughout the entire pregnancy. In fact, I was able to put on my normal clothes just about a week after she came. She and I both looked like we had been through a war. She began to struggle with her bilirubin numbers, and was not cleared to be released from the hospital. Wednesday slipped into Thursday, Thursday turned to Friday, and still her numbers were climbing. I was given one last day to stay in the hospital per my insurance that Friday night, and kept arguing with everyone about the fact that I had no intention of going home and leaving Sara behind. Saturday morning came, and they drew bloodwork yet again. Her tiny heels were so bruised from all the sticks. For the first time, her numbers had not gotten higher. They were the same as the evening before, but still far above normal. They were threatening to place her under the purple lights, and I knew that once that process began it would be four or even five days before she would be able to be released. I wanted to nurse her, and knew that separation would likely mean that had to stop. I began to negotiate with the doctor, and he finally agreed to let me take her home, as long as I was positively sure I could bring her back within a twelve-hour window to get her blood drawn again. We walked out of the hospital at 7:30 that evening, and I took Sara home to meet her big sister.

Saturday night was tough. Sara was very fussy and unhappy, and I began to question my determination to bring her home against their advice. We were literally up all night. Only Jessica slept. Very early on Sunday morning, we realized we were out of milk, and Gary told me he would run down to Walgreens, which was open 24 hours a day, and pick some up. He walked out the front door. Almost at the same time, my phone rang. It was my mother asking how things were going and if I needed any help getting Sara back to the hospital for her blood test.

I told her that Gary had just run to the store, and that he was coming back to take Sara, and I was going to stay at home and let Jessica sleep. I was not cleared to drive yet, so that plan seemed like the best one to us. I hung up the phone, and was quite surprised, and then upset, to hear my mother knocking on my front door about fifteen minutes later.

I opened the door, and she was standing there, holding a gallon of milk. She quietly said she was just going to wait with me until Gary got back. I became upset as I realized she was suggesting that he might not actually be returning. I told her she needed to support me, and Gary, and stop expecting the worst from him.

We sat together, and the time began to slip by. It was getting to the point that I knew if we did not start towards the hospital, Sara would be outside the window of time to get her bloodwork properly done. It was cold that morning. My mother finally stood up, and just began to bundle Sara up. She drove her out to the hospital, and the blood work was completed. Sara's numbers had dropped slightly so they formally released her, and my mother brought her back to me.

It would be ten days before the phone would ring, Gary's voice on the other end. He said, "How's it going?"

I said, "Did they move Walgreens?"

He replied, "As I was driving there, I just realized I can't do this anymore. I love Valerie. She needs me. You are strong. You will be alright. I tried to pretend that it would be OK because I thought it would be cheaper to stay with you and pay her for one, than to stay with her and pay you for two. But the truth is I want to be with her. So that is where I have been."

The floor tipped again as the full realization hit me like a truck plowing off of a bridge and smashing into the water below it. I had to own the fact that I had allowed him back into our lives, and he had once again betrayed us in the worst possible way. That it was truly over, and there was no respite this time. We were on our own.

Life was too busy to spend much time grieving. Actually, I know that I put the grieving process off, and did eventually have to deal with it later. The lesson I learned was that it was not possible to skip it. No matter how busy I was, or how much I tried to silence the voices in my head, the process of grieving demanded my attention to move through it later in my life.

In 1987, the law required employers to give you six weeks of maternity leave. Exactly six weeks, no more, no less. It was up to the boss to determine if you could take additional time off. I called my boss, and asked if I could be given two additional days off, with no pay. Since Sara was born on a Wednesday, I knew that the additional Thursday and Friday, coupled with the two days of the weekend, would mean the world to us. I found myself incredulous when my supervisor told me that if I did not return on Thursday, I would be let go. I have remembered the way that felt from that moment to this one.

Feeling totally out of control of my life, terrified I would not be able to make my bills if I did stand up and say I had no idea how I could return that day. I vowed to be empathetic and supportive should I ever be in a position where I had to supervise others.

The time flew by and before long I was standing on the precipice of the dreaded week. The evening before my first day back, I organized two diaper bags, secured two car seats into my Ford Tempo, and spent a fitful night getting up to nurse Sara, and calm Jessica when she was disturbed by us. I spent most of the morning tending to the girls, and happy for the distraction as the time to report to my job was creeping closer. Finally, in the early afternoon, I headed to my Aunt and Uncle's house, and prepared to leave my children for the rest of the day.

My Aunt Reva and Uncle Sam were in their eighties at this point in time. I had always been close to them throughout my life, and reached out to ask them about babysitting the girls when my maternity leave was over. They readily agreed, and did it for absolutely no charge. It was such a blessing to me to have their support. The truth is, I could not have afforded to pay for childcare, and I had no desire to leave such young children in the care of anyone I did not know really well. I knew they would be well cared for at Reva and Sam's home, and loved beyond measure. It was the only thing that made leaving them bearable.

The first weeks were difficult, but as they slipped by, I fell into a routine of sorts. I had help a few nights a week. My mother would pick the girls up after she finished working and took them to my place and put them to bed so on those evenings all I had to do was drive home. My younger sister came over and helped with the girls when my Aunt and Uncle were not available. It truly took a village, and my family stepped in. My older sister consistently gave me clothes that her daughter had outgrown, so I had that resource as well. Gary's parents picked the girls up often for part of the weekend, which allowed me to rest.

The weather was now warm, and there was one wonderful Sunday afternoon when I realized everything was going to be OK. I had managed to make it to church, and afterwards, drove to a local nursery to buy petunias to put in a vase on my tiny front porch. I had put both girls down for a nap, and as I planted the flowers, and felt the sun on my face, I had an overwhelming sense of peace. It was as if God himself was reaching out to me with the assurance that the future was going to take care of itself. For the first time in nearly a year, I felt positive again, and cautiously hopeful. I was making it, one day at a time. The lesson I was being taught was how to experience gratitude, and be thankful for what was going right, instead of focusing on the pieces that were out of place.

As summer began to draw to a close, I was presented with an opportunity to be promoted to the special procedures area of the hospital where I worked. This presented several awesome aspects, and some very real challenges. It would be an hourly pay increase, and the opportunity to make additional money because it required me to be on call a few times a month. It also would mean working first shift, so my time to report to work would be 7am.

I turned it down at first. The position remained open another few weeks. A supervisor came to me, and said, "Are you SURE you don't want to accept this role?"

I decided it must be meant for me, and simply took a big leap and agreed to the change. Looking back, it is now obvious why I was headed back to the famous room 9. That was where Evan was working. Without knowing it then, I had made a decision that would again change the course of my life forever.

Evan was tall, handsome, and kind. He remains, to this day, the most gifted special procedures technologist I have ever seen. He was one of the leaders in the group in room 9. A favorite of the doctors, and someone who had clearly found work that he was born to do.

A sadness surrounded Evan, though. He seemed lonely, and distracted. I learned through co-workers that he had just come through a divorce. The same as me. He had two very young daughters. The same as me. He also was the partner who was left. The same as me.

I used to watch him work, and wonder how anyone would decide to leave him. I often thought what I would give to have a husband who wanted to be with me, and was devoted to my children. When Gary departed, he left completely. He did not want to be given any visiting rights. Instead, I reached out to his parents, and they eagerly spent that time with the girls. Evan, on the other hand, rarely spoke of anything personal that did not involve his girls, and when he could see them next. I still remember the day that he pulled pictures of Christy and Jenny out of his wallet, and showed them to me. They were 4 and 2. I returned the gesture by pulling pictures of my girls out of my wallet, who were then 5 months and nearly 2 years old. One day I said, "It's hard, isn't it?" I did not elaborate on what I was talking about. I knew he would know. He just looked at me, with that pain in his eyes, and said, "It is so hard."

I allowed myself to think, just occasionally, about what a similar history Evan and I shared. We had the same profession. We had come through the same heart-breaking personal journey at the same exact time. We both loved our girls beyond measure. And we both were broken, and sad. There was a level of understanding between us that developed very early in our friendship, and was just our unspoken language.

Evan slowly began to be intentional about our friendship. I had been assigned to another technologist to get oriented to room 8. That was not going so well. David was intimidating, and often felt the need to quiz me in front of others, which only increased my anxiousness. Working in special procedures is a huge responsibility, as often the sickest of patients are in need of those procedures. I also was running on empty due to lack of enough sleep with such small children at home. One particularly taxing day, David was asking me to quickly perform a conversion and figure out the percentage of heparin that was injected into a saline bag. We both thought we were alone in the exam room, until a voice from the control booth quietly, but forcefully, said, "David, that's enough. We both know that isn't anything she will ever have to do."

It was Evan.

I saw David's color begin to drain from his face. Evan then walked up to the two of us and said, "I will take it from here. For the rest of the orientation, she's going to be with me."

Life immediately brightened for me. Evan was an excellent teacher. He was able to explain things in simple terms, and inspire confidence in my belief and ability to do the job. Our friendship grew.

Life was getting ready to throw me another dark chapter. My grandfather, who was a widower, got sick, and was taken to the hospital. He was there just a short time. I visited twice, and he was in good spirits. I still remember debating about visiting him a third time, but made the decision to go to the grocery store instead while I had time. It would prove to be a decision I would regret for years. I received a call, and learned that the evening I skipped visiting him, he suffered a massive heart attack, and died instantly. I was filled with grief, and remorse. Once again, my mother would be the voice of reason for me. She said, "Kim, he knew how much you loved him. He would understand that you needed to go to the grocery store while you had someone to watch the girls. Everything is going to be OK."

I was assigned to be on call for work the day of my grandfather's funeral. I was trying to figure out how to juggle that issue, when I received a call from work to let me know that Evan had asked about me, and had changed his schedule to cover my call. Therefore, that burden was lifted. The day of the funeral, I received a card in the mail that I would carry with me for years. It was from Evan, and had a message that read, "there are people that care for you much more than you know." Even in my sadness, my heart skipped a beat. I wondered to myself if it was a message that was more than one of sympathy for my grandfather's death. I allowed myself to start to consider that maybe I was not going to be alone for the rest of my life. I found myself looking down at my hands and asking God if one day I would again see a ring that would symbolize my deep connection to someone else.

Meanwhile, life raced on at breakneck speed.

There was a departmental softball team. Evan was on it. I never went to the games, but near the end of the summer, there was a poster put up in the break room that announced an end of the season party the next weekend. It was at the house of a co-worker who lived very close to my townhouse. Evan signed the poster indicating his intention to go to the party. I signed my name right under his. In addition, I had to come to terms with the fact that I was going to have to acknowledge that I wanted to explore something beyond a friendship more than I wanted to remain paralyzed by the fear of being rejected.

I pulled together a few dollars and went shopping. I so clearly remember going to a discount rate store, and trying on jeans and shirts. I finally settled on an outfit I liked, and then at the cash register splurged and bought new earrings. They were classic eighties style...big and chunky, made out of fabric with a plaid pattern on them. Coupled with my new perm, I was feeling very confident, and carefully laid my clothes out in preparation for the party. I told my mother and younger sister about Evan, and my hopes for the party to be a launching pad for growing closer. Gary's parents asked to pick the girls up and keep them overnight that Saturday, which I took as a sign from the universe that I was destined to be free to explore this budding relationship.

I drove to the party with butterflies in my stomach. I enjoyed my time with my friends, and was really happy to see Evan arrive. One of his best friends, and our fellow co-worker, John, was also there with his wife, Linda. As the night wore on, I found myself sitting out back with them. At one point, we ran out of beer, and I told them there was a convenience store not far up the street. That we could walk there if they wanted more.

Evan, John, and I started toward the store. I realized quickly that I had underestimated how many blocks away the store actually was. We laughed and laughed as we walked that warm evening. I did not want the walk to end. It was fun to feel young again, and to laugh so hard, I had to stop and double over at times. We made it to the store, and back to the party, and I hated to see the night end.

It grew late, and it was time to go. I devised a plan to spend more time with Evan. I told him I was a little uncomfortable driving home alone so late, and asked if he would follow me to my townhouse around the corner. He agreed.

He was right behind me in his dark brown Thunderbird. I spent more time looking into the rear view mirror than watching the road. My butterflies had returned in force. I was about to take a big risk, and reveal how I was feeling.

When I pulled into my garage, Evan backed up and turned the car around to go back down the drive. I walked up to the side of his car, and he powered the window down. I said, "My girls are gone for the night. Would you maybe want to come in for a drink, or to talk?"

To this day, I cannot explain how mortified I was when his response was, "I really can't. I am going to go fishing with my Dad tomorrow, so I have an early morning. I better get home."

He powered the window up, and then pulled down the long drive. I sat down on my little porch, next to my petunias, and watched him waiting to pull out. It was quite late, and there was not any traffic to speak of. He sat there. And sat there. And sat there. I began to wonder if he had forgotten which way to turn to get back to the highway, and wondered how I could possibly face him again if he drove back up the drive. Slowly, slowly, slowly, his turn signal came on, and he made the correct right turn and disappeared into the night.

I was struck that night by the difference that had happened between when I had left for the party, and when I returned. I took the plaid earrings off and considered throwing them away. My new outfit suddenly seemed all wrong. I laid down, and slept very little. Sunday found me feeling very low. My mother called, and I told her I had a swing and a giant miss. My sister called as well. Both of them were sympathetic. I actually went out and bought a paper to look at the job ads to see if any other hospital in the area was hiring.

I also realized that Monday morning was coming, and I had no choice except to go back to work. I was so unhappy with myself for pushing things to move beyond what I clearly believed was more than Evan wanted. I was certain I had jeopardized our friendship by being so bold as to invite him into my place.

Then, as I was sitting in my sackcloth and ashes, completely immersed in a pity party, I had a bright spot emerge. I remembered that I had agreed to work second shift the next day. Which meant that I could delay seeing Evan until Tuesday! All I had to do was go in and lay low until the room 8 folks were finished at 3. Hallelujah! I could delay dealing with my misstep. I could figure out a way to salvage our friendship and return to the status quo.

I had a rudimentary plan. I thought I might say something along the lines that we had so much fun, that the last part of the night was fuzzy....and to thank him for being so nice to be sure I got home. To pretend that I did not remember asking him in, and being turned down for fishing!

I rounded the familiar corner to walk into the department and there he sat. He was not in room 9. He was at the front desk. Damn! I tried to bump up my speech, since I obviously had to deliver it now, and did not have the additional day I had anticipated.

Before I could do that, though, Evan said, "Hey, Saturday was fun! A bunch of us are going to the end-of-the-summer fireworks next weekend. Do you want to go?"

I fumbled through saying, yes, I would like to go. He seemed happy, and got up and left. I worked that shift thoroughly confused.

It would be the next day before my confusion lifted. Evan called me and said he was free all weekend, not just the Sunday of the fireworks, and wanted to know if I would like to hang out. I said, "Do you mean, like a date?" To which he replied, "Yeah. Like a date. I meant that when I asked you to go to the fireworks."

I heard myself blurt out that my little sister had given me passes to King's Island, the local amusement park, and they were about to close for the season. He said how much fun that would be, and we made plans to go that next Saturday to the park, and to the fireworks on Sunday, and hung up. It was a bit surreal for me to go into work the next several days. Evan seemed happier. I was cautious and confused.

I went home and called my mother and little sister to share the news that maybe I did not need to throw away my plaid earrings after all. I was not sure what was happening, exactly, but that things definitely were looking up. I was celebrating, all the way to the next morning, which found me waking up to a dead car battery. I called work to say I would be late, and took a cab in.

Evan came forward again, and asked how I was getting home. I told him my mother was with my girls, and I was trying to figure out how to get my car serviced. He offered to take me home and look at my car.

This vivid memory is of me walking into my townhouse. Jessica was toddling around the living room. Sara was laying on a blanket on the floor. My mom was sitting in a rocking chair that was upholstered with blue pineapples. I introduced Evan to her, and when he looked the other way, she looked at me, and sent the clear message, "WOW!" Without saying a word.

Evan went immediately to the girls. Talking to Jessie, and sitting on the floor next to Sara. He helped me straighten out the battery issue and got me back on the road. He then left, but asked what I was doing the Friday before the Saturday at the theme park, before the fireworks on Sunday. He said that it was his weekend to be apart from his girls, and since we were both off call duty, maybe we could just get together that night too. I couldn't know it then, but it became a routine that we would share for years to come....having a weekend with four little girls that we cared for and loved, and then a weekend where we both shared our children with other family, given a few short days to be alone to build our relationship.

Friday arrived, and we made BIG plans. We decided we would order pizza, and watch, The Golden Child, a movie we both liked and that he had on tape. He arrived, I put my girls to bed, and we popped the movie into my shiny Beta machine.

When I moved to my new townhouse, my father, who was literally the king of the flea market, took a couple hundred dollars, and found pieces of furniture for me so I was not living in bare rooms. One of his finds was a really big, white couch. Evan and I sat down on the couch, happy to be munching on our pizza.

During that time period of my life, I was chronically tired, because it was nearly impossible to get enough sleep with an infant, a toddler, and a demanding job that began at 7a.m. each morning. I found myself feeling sleepy, despite how excited I was to have Evan there, and our weekend plans. More than once I got up and made an excuse to walk into the kitchen area to try to wake myself up. At some point, I lost my battle, and fell asleep.

What happened next still melts my heart. I awoke to hear Sara cooing and assumed I was hearing her next to me in the bedroom we shared. It took me a minute to orient myself that I was downstairs, instead of in my bedroom on the second floor. I was stretched completely out on my big, white couch, laying on my stomach. When I opened my eyes I saw Evan, sitting just a few feet away, in the rocking chair with the blue pineapples. He was holding Sara, and giving her the 3a.m. bottle that she needed since she was still so very small. At first, I thought I was dreaming, and then I slowly sat up. I looked at Evan in amazement, and just fumbled through asking what in the world he was doing.

He simply said, "You fell asleep. You were so tired. I guess I fell asleep too, after I moved over here to the rocking chair so you could have the couch. I was only going to watch the end of the movie, but woke up a little while ago. I heard Sara wake up and begin to fuss, and I knew she needed her bottle. You told me last night when you were getting her bottles ready for tomorrow that she still took a bottle in the middle of the night. I hope it is OK. I just went up and got her, and thought I could feed her, and let you sleep. I really hope you are not upset with me. I was just trying to help, not overstep."

My mind reeled.

I could not imagine that this man, who was more or less still a stranger to me, and totally new in my daughter's lives, would do this on his Friday night. Would actually want to do this. He looked so at peace, and totally at home. Sara was completely comfortable, and he finished feeding her, burped her like an expert, and took her back up to her crib. I continued to sit on the couch and watch the whole thing unfold as if I was a character in a play.

When he reemerged at the bottom of the stairs, he said, "I better get going home and check on things there. I will be back tomorrow around noon, so we can head to King's Island!"

I got up and walked the short distance to the front door. I put my arms around him, and just stood there for a while. It was very quiet. I could hear the tick tock of my wall clock. I could not help myself, and finally asked what I had wondered about for days and days. Why had he turned me down just the weekend before, and sat for such a long time at the bottom of the driveway afterwards?

He was so sheepish, and so adorable all at the same time. He looked at the floor a minute, and then shifted his weight from foot to foot. He finally said, "I honestly was going fishing with my Dad that next morning. It did not even occur to me that you might like me that way until I rolled up the window and turned around and headed down the drive. All of a sudden I thought, OH MY GOD! She just asked you in, and you just turned her down! So I sat there for the longest time, thinking maybe I could come back and knock on the door. But by then I figured you were inside, and headed to bed, and I felt really dumb, so I finally headed home. And then I spent Sunday figuring out how I would make it right on Monday at work."

I just stared at him. And then the air got heavy, and time suspended as he bent down and kissed me for the first time. It was a small kiss, and yet somehow it changed everything forever. It felt brand new, and like coming home to someplace I had never been before at the same time.

He left. And I went upstairs to bed. I drifted into a peaceful sleep, the girls both slept for a long while, which was not the norm on any given night. We all seemed to understand that things had just gotten better in the most important way possible.

Saturday morning, Gary's parents came and picked up Jessica and Sara. They were always so happy to see the girls, and the girls were always just ecstatic to see them. I sent them out the door, barely able to contain my excitement. I also felt guilty. I mean, how could it be right, that I was getting ready to explore something for myself? I believed that my first commitment had to be to them at all times. A lesson learned as things transpired was that if I took care of myself, I was always much more able to take care of them, too.

Before long, the doorbell rang. Evan stood there, in his Banana Republic tee shirt and shorts, with a small bouquet of flowers in his hand. The sun was shining, and the same car I watched pull away a short week before was parked in my driveway. I put the flowers in some water, and we headed for a magical day at the amusement park.

It began with small things. Just being comfortable in spaces of silence during the drive there was so pleasant. The casual way he reached over to hold my hand, which made me know that somehow this was meant to be. It was so much fun, just walking out in the sunshine, through a place I had been so many times, which was so familiar to me, and yet brand new all at once now that Evan was there.

He kept saying, "You give new meaning to standing in line!" Because as we stood waiting for our turn, it gave us an opportunity to talk, and he would occasionally place his arm around my waist. I became aware that we were behaving like one of those yucky couples who were falling head over heels for one another. I did not care one bit.

Towards the end of the day, we decided to ride a water feature, and as we splashed through it, we got absolutely soaked. At one point, Evan was laughing so hard, I thought he was not going to be able to catch his breath. I remember thinking it had probably been a good, long while since he had felt so carefree. I could relate. For that day, time seemed to suspend itself, and we were able to be just two people falling in love.

The night fell, the fireworks were sent up, and it was time to go home. It was a quiet ride back. Evan reached into his glove compartment, and pulled out a cassette tape. He quietly said, "I made this for you. I hope that is alright."

Song after song played as we drove. Blood, Sweat, and Tears' song, "You Made Me So Very Happy" was among them. It was clear to me that I was right where I belonged.

It was truly déjà vu as we approached my townhouse, and once again, I asked if he would like to come in. This time, there was not any talk of needing to get up early the next day to go fishing. This time, Evan parked, and walked in with me. We stood there together, and did not even ask one another what the next steps were. We knew. In an unspoken shorthand that had developed so quickly and easily between us.

I went upstairs, and looked at myself in the mirror, and stared deep into my own eyes and asked myself one last time if I was sure this was right. I thought about our four little girls, who hung in the balance of any decisions we made. I knew this was not the regular dating scenario. We were not playing for a weekend. We had both come through too much to be foolish. We both were also still very vulnerable, and sensitive to the fact that what we each thought could never happen, did happen, and how hard that road had been. Neither of us wanted to ever walk it again.

It did not take too long for me to decide it was worth the risk to move forward. I lit some candles, and changed into a robe, and walked down the stairs holding a small candle in my hand. I just stood at the bottom of the stairs, and looked at Evan who was sitting across the room on the couch. He got up, and asked one question. "Are you sure?" I just nodded yes, and he took my hand and we climbed the staircase together. The depth of satisfaction that we experienced together that night was as profound as the depth of loneliness and heartbreak each had experienced alone. It was warm, and sweet, and so intimate. The bond that was forged was one that ended up being one that would never be truly broken.

The next day found us going to the end of the summer fireworks extravaganza down on the Ohio River banks. As the sky lit up, we stood in a throng of hundreds of thousands of people, and somehow were all alone, just the two of us together. We were a couple. And we each knew it. We were stronger, and happier, together. Another night was spent in the new wonderful space we had created, and then the holiday weekend was over.

Evan went home, my girls were dropped back off, and life fell back into a familiar routine. My phone rang, and Evan asked if I wanted him to bring over, some of the now famous fish, he had caught with his father, to fry for dinner. I agreed, and as I gave the girls their evening bath, Evan happily made dinner downstairs. It was all so easy, falling into a new normal. He went home that night, because we had discussed the gravity of exposing our children to our relationship before we were completely certain where we were going. Although it seemed a given, it was all still so new, neither of us were ready to have our children experience waking up with both of us at the breakfast table.

When I walked into the specials department the next day, Evan was waiting for me. He pushed me backwards into the changing room, and closed, and locked the door behind us. He said, "I just couldn't wait to see you today!" We stood and held one another.

I thought how much better Christmas was going to be that year, compared to the one just a little less than a year before. I thanked God for this new pathway, and learned the lesson that it really is always darkest before the dawn.

Chapter 9 (1988) Becoming a Wife Again and a Stepmother for the First Time

Somewhere, out there, beneath the pale moonlight, someone's thinking of me, and loving me tonight. Somewhere, out there, someone's saying a prayer. That we'll find one another, somewhere out there, out where dreams come true~Somewhere Out There, Linda Ronstandt

Life moved at a frenetic pace for Evan and me, as we officially became a couple. At the age of twenty-four, I found myself regularly caring for four little girls, all under the age of five. Most of our activities focused on our children. We both were so grateful for the life we were putting together. It was not without hurdles, however.

Not everyone was happy to see us together. As soon as I was settled into a routine with Evan, flowers began to arrive from Gary, with crazy notes that said how much he was thinking of me. There was bitterness on both sides with respect to our former spouses, and their extended families. It took a lot of work to try to embrace the positive, and compartmentalize the animosity that at times reared its ugly head. We tried to keep the girls out of it, but that was also challenging. Looking back, I marvel at how much we did handle at such a relatively young age. It was unchartered territory for both of us.

As the spring approached, I began to think seriously about trying to purchase a home, and move out of my rented townhouse. I turned to my mother for advice, and as usual, she did not disappoint. She told me that I could buy a two-family home, and use the rent from the second unit to apply towards the mortgage in the eyes of the bank. And it worked! As May ended, I found myself moving into a fixer-upper on a nice street in Fort Thomas. I have literally never before, or since, seen so much wallpaper in one place.

It was exhausting, and a lot of fun to work on the house. At one point, I lifted up a tile in the dropped ceiling in the kitchen, and discovered that someone had painted the windows black above it so light did not shine down through it. Down came the dropped ceiling, and the paint was removed from the windows, doubling them in size. It felt like an endless mission to discover what else was buried with bad remodeling.

Evan and I had not really spoken about getting married. We also intuitively knew we were going to be together going forward. One day, prior to the purchase of my house, I had a very direct conversation with Evan about the future, and told him I was moving ahead so that I could have more financial security in my future. He happily worked with me on my house, and before long, it just became apparent that we were pulling in the same direction in our personal and professional lives, and we tiptoed out into the waters to discuss how getting married would change things, and how our children fit into the picture.

June arrived, and so did a shiny engagement ring. We set the date for the following March.

As the summer continued, we put Evan's house on the market to sell. It made sense for us to begin together in the new place that we were working so hard to remodel. Piece by piece we built our new home, and I treasured every item we acquired.

As the fall drew close, we experienced some significant stress around dealing with issues that involved Gary. Evan would go with me to court hearings, but he did not have a voice. At one point, my father said, "You know, if you got married now, he would be able to speak at these hearings as your husband, and that would make a difference."

Evan and I looked at one another, and our girls, and then at the calendar. We decided to move the wedding date up. I jokingly told Evan that if I was going to actually do this again, I had better get a fabulous trip out of it. Like maybe even to Hawaii.

We originally picked Saturday, November 12, 1988 as the new date. One day Evan showed up and said he had changed his mind about that after all. My stomach did a little cartwheel. He then burst into a big grin, and said we had to move the wedding to Friday, November 11, 1988. Why? He had been working with a travel agent, and our honeymoon was going to be a cruise through the Hawaiian Islands, and we had to fly out on Saturday, November 12th in order to catch the boat!

It was a happy, exciting time. I went once again to the bridal department in search of the perfect dress. As it turned out, it was on display, on a mannequin, right at the entrance of the bridal department. It was a beautiful shade of pink, with sleeves as big as my permed, eighties-style hair. It was the perfect dress to start my new life in. I then went to the department store and found four perfect, pink dresses for our four beautiful girls. Everything raced towards us. We were so much in love.

During that year, "An American Tail" always seemed to be playing on our VCR. It was the story of a young mouse named Fievel Mousekewitz. Fievel's family decided to emigrate from Russia to America, but a storm ensued, and Fievel was separated from his family as a result. He was terrified, but made his way to America on his own, and the rest of the story focuses on the quest he and his family went on to be reunited. There is a beautiful song in the middle of it, while they are still separated, that finds Fievel and his mother both staring out the window at the moon. The lyrics include, "And even though I know how far apart we are, it helps to think we might be wishing on the same bright star. And when the night wind starts to sing a lonesome lullaby, it helps to think we're sleeping underneath the same big sky. Somewhere out there, if love can see us through, then we'll be together. Somewhere out there, out where dreams come true."

I came through the family room one day to find Jessica rocking in her little chair, watching that movie, crying so hard. Alarmed, I asked what was wrong. She replied, "It is just so sad that he can't find his mommy and he is all alone!" I assured her if she watched it until the end, there would be a happy reunion.

Silly as it may sound, that turned out to be the song that we decided was perfect for us to play as I walked down the aisle to stand with Evan at the wedding ceremony. Since the girls were so young, we had each of our mothers walk up the aisle holding their granddaughters' hands. For the second time, my father walked me up the aisle towards my future. My sisters stood at my side, and Evan had his brother and best friend stand with him. It was a simple, beautiful, special service.

Shortly before the wedding service, I made my way into a room in the church alone, and stood looking at myself in the mirror for several minutes. I thought about how lucky I was. I said a prayer to ask for blessings to follow our marriage. I was deliberate in my decision to marry Evan, and determined that nothing would ever come between us.

I could not have known it then, but many joys and many sorrows were ahead of us. The lesson I learned throughout all of it was there are some questions that have no answers, and some bridges you just cannot cross. Later, this wedding would be nicknamed, Version 1.0 by our minister, Gerald. To understand why, I have to take you twenty-nine years into the future. A lot happens between now and then.

Chapter 10 (1991) Having a Son

What are little boys made of? Frogs and snails and puppy-dogs' tails. That's what little boys are made of.~Nursery Rhyme
Look Harder. Simba you have forgotten me. You have forgotten who you are and so forgotten me. Look inside yourself, Simba. You are more than what you have become. You must take your place in the circle of life. Remember who you are. You are my son, and the one true king. Remember who you are. Remember. Remember. Remember.~The Lion King

We were not married very long before we decided we wanted to add more children to our family. We loved our girls, they loved each other, and we literally built our world around them. We battled with the fact that our girls were adversely affected by the bitterness from each of our divorces. We did our best.

We renewed our resolve to move forward, and create the future we wanted for ourselves and our children. We believed that our family was incomplete, and that sharing the birth of a child would add a special level of intimacy and closeness to our union. Therefore, we decided we would try to conceive.

The pathway was not easy. I remember thinking more than once how ironic it was that I was so able to conceive in my previous marriage, with a man who did not want to stay married to me. Only to find myself in a marriage with a man who was totally devoted to me, and yet we could not easily get pregnant. Evan submitted to a surgical procedure to reverse the vasectomy he had before he met me. The results were not enough to conceive without intervention. That was when we turned to a local doctor who had a wonderful reputation for helping couples who were struggling to build their families.

I could not have known it then, but the journey we were about to embark on was going to be very difficult. Moreover, expensive. In order to overcome the challenges from the vasectomy and subsequent reversal, our new doctor recommended artificial insemination. It was not covered by insurance. It also required an intensive amount of artificial hormones to manipulate things that would allow the procedure to be successful. All of that was coupled with driving to the doctor's office two times a month to have the uncomfortable . procedure performed, and then the excruciating wait to see, day-by-day, if it was successful.

Month after month came and went. There was no success. We tried to remain optimistic, and looking back, now understand what a toll it took on our relationship from an emotional, physical, and financial standpoint. About the time that we were ready to give up, I noticed the familiar signs of feeling pregnant. It was December, a long, seven months into the process, and we simply held our breath. I bought a home pregnancy test, and was thrilled to see that it came back positive. Our excitement was very short lived.

Within a week, I miscarried. Our doctor was empathetic, and tried to console me by saying that this happened many times, to many women. That most women do not even realize it because they are not monitoring every signal every day the way we were. I told him I was ready to give up.

He looked at me and said, "You are one of the lucky ones in my practice. Most of the women I treat do not know if they can even get pregnant. You know you can, and that you can carry a baby through to delivery. If you quit now, you have no chance of growing your family."

A powerful lesson. He gave me a whole new way to reframe and think about everything.

As it turned out, I did return the following month for another round of artificial insemination treatments. This time, the familiar signs returned. I suspected I was pregnant, but was hesitant to reach out and learn if it was true. I waited. One week turned into another. Finally, my doctor's office called because I had not been to my scheduled appointments. I went in the following day. The pregnancy test was positive, and I spent a few more weeks afraid that at any given moment it would be taken away from me. It proved to be a worry that I did not need to have.

Month after month passed. Many people in our lives were happy for us. Others thought we had lost our minds. We were so excited for the future and what it all would mean for our growing family. We set about remodeling our home to include a small nursery. I went to work at my new job. We made the decision to wait to find out the sex of the baby until the day the baby was born.

One day, at the hospital during my shift, I was overcome with curiosity. I slipped into the ultrasound room, and a good friend scanned my very large belly. Our eyes locked as she broke into a huge grin. I had been jokingly referring to my unborn baby as Louise. My friend told me I was going to have to alter that plan. She then broke into the song, "Louie, Louie," and told me that I was carrying a boy.

My world was rocked. I could not wait to get home and tell Evan that we were going to experience something new on every level.

We had great fun that spring and summer getting a small nursery together to welcome our baby boy. For months, we debated names. I wanted to name him after his father, as a namesake. Evan was not excited about that idea at all. It actually came right down to the time that he was born, and we saw him, that Evan said he thought he would like to do that. Almost immediately, we began to refer to him as Ej. For Evan, Junior.

Ej fit into our family in such an easy way. It was as if he was always supposed to be with us. He was a happy, sunny-dispositioned child. There was a natural curiosity about him, and he loved to learn. His sisters doted on him, and we fell into an easy routine with our newest addition.

I could not imagine how life could be better. I also could not imagine the lessons I would have to learn as the world literally disintegrated before us. Later, we were forced to turn loose of the son we were so happy to welcome into the world. It would be a slow, excruciating descent into mental illness, drug addiction, and behaviors that became so dangerous it tore away at the very fabric of our family's existence. It would inevitably teach me that, no matter how tightly you hold onto something, it can be taken away from you. There would be many, many happy years between now and that terrible day, however.

Chapter 11 (1996) Elvis' Birthday, the Snowstorm of the Century and Absolute Absence of Sleep

The two most important days in your life are the day you are born and the day you find out why~Mark Twain

The years seemed to go by faster and faster as our children grew. Evan's job had taken him into a new dimension. He left the hospital setting to join a company as a medical sales representative. Travelling became a normal part of his routine, and he was gone more and more. And more. I did not understand it at the time, but we were learning to live separate lives with such frequent, and prolonged, separations. I had no idea what he was going through, and he honestly had no idea what my life was like at home when he was away. One night, he called home, complaining about eating alone at the hotel restaurant. After yet another day of holding everything together, and wishing I had just one moment to myself without the demands of one of our children, I snapped at him, "I am REALLY sorry this is so bad for YOU"………I could imagine nothing better than having an uninterrupted meal.

It would be years before I had a position that required that I travel, and experience the innate loneliness that happens when the workday ends. Another lesson learned.

Evan and I faced a difficult decision in the spring of 1995. His company had reorganized, and he was one of the people who was not phased out. That was the good news. The bad news was that his new role came with a different territory that took him out of Kentucky. We made the difficult decision to move away, to Nashville, TN, to accept the opportunity, leaving friends and family, most notably, Christy and Jenny.

By the spring of 1995, we had an enormous surprise. I discovered I was pregnant again. This time, things seemed different, and it would take a while to understand why. As the school year ended, we notified the teachers that our other children would be transferring to a school in Nashville for the fall. Tears were shed. Parties were held, and gifts were plentiful. I went through the process of taking them out of the system, in preparation for the transition. It was a difficult time for all of us.

At the time that Evan received the offer to relocate, we were very naïve about the process. We did not get everything in writing, signed and sealed, and that became a very painful lesson down the road. We were told to place our house on the market, and that in the event it did not sell, the company would buy it so we could move without incident. That did not happen after all.

We spent the summer living in a corporate apartment, replete with a swimming pool, feeling very much as if we were on vacation. There was one wonderful day when Sara jumped into the pool, and swam to the deep end and back without any use of a flotation device. It was sunny, and we felt like we were on a grand adventure, looking forward to what the future had in store. I was experiencing problems with my pregnancy, which concerned us, but was not to the point of sounding alarm bells. Our house was on the market in Kentucky, and we spent two weeks in July across my birthday in St. Thomas. Things seemed to be in place.

When we arrived in St. Thomas, Ej immediately struck up a conversation with a cab driver, named, Sam, and he became the person who drove us for the remainder of our time there. We had a private beach available to us, and we took many pictures on Morning Star Beach as our time there together progressed. It was a wonderful time that bonded us together as a family, which was why the future that found us torn apart was just that much more painful.

While in Nashville, we went under contract to build a house. I spent hours with Evan picking out shingle colors, and choosing just the right floor plan. We were thrilled with the house as it went up brick by brick, and we drove by nearly daily to see the progress. It was in just the right school district. We were sure we were on track. What could go wrong?

Our house in Kentucky did not sell. What I have now come to believe as divine intervention occurred. It made no sense that the house stood there, with no offers, month after month. We turned to Evan's manager, and relayed the message that we needed to take advantage of the offer to have the company buy the house so we could move forward and close on our new home in Nashville. We were stunned, and saddened by the response.

He simply replied that the reorganization had not been as successful as they had hoped, the numbers were off, and the gentleman's agreement to purchase our home was off the table. We were on our own.

Evan and I looked at each other. We looked at our bank account. We looked at the fact that I was now very pregnant, and was experiencing major issues with carrying this new baby to term. We struggled. We fought. We cried. We tried to decide if what was happening was a test to jump off the cliff and trust that everything would work out the right way. We had no capacity to pay our mortgage in Kentucky as well as the new house payment in Nashville beyond three months. Should we jump, and trust that God would provide? Should we figure out a new path?

I could not take on additional work as I was essentially told to be on bed rest at that point to avoid losing the baby I was carrying.

The day of reckoning came. Evan and I sat together on the steps of our home in Kentucky as he explained to me that he simply could not sign for a second home, and risk losing both of them if the ninety days ran out and our house did not sell.

My heart fell. I saw all of the plans and months of picking out carpet and counter top choices turning into a useless exercise. We called the real estate agent in Nashville, and told her about our latest development. She told us that she had a couple who wanted to move into the new neighborhood, but had no desire to wait to build. They would be likely candidates to purchase our newly completed home.

Heartbroken, I signed the paperwork with Evan. Someone else was going to enjoy the home we had designed. It also meant that Evan was going to take an apartment in Nashville Monday through Friday, and I was going back to our home in Kentucky with the children to live essentially as a single mother throughout the week.

Evan took a room in a terrible part of town to save money. This was in an era that predated texting and social media, so we were essentially separated once he drove away each week. I re-enrolled the children in school, and awkwardly asked if I should return the going away gifts they had all received just three months before.

As the school year began, the children fell into a familiar routine. Their friends were happy to see they were back in school. Our family was happy to see that we were not actually going to move away. We would not be leaving Christy and Jenni.

I was scared, and sad, and felt so alone each Sunday night as Evan departed. It was difficult each week to meet the needs of the children on my own. I also was unable to do what my doctor recommended, and rest. The complications with my pregnancy mounted.

I was hospitalized several times to stop premature contractions. Evan would head down the road each Sunday night. As the fall progressed, he had a habit of calling me as he stopped for gas along the way to see if the contractions I was having were getting better, or worse, so he knew what to do. Head on to Nashville, or turn around and race home?

We made it to Christmas break. Our new baby was due the first week of January, so after months of intervention, we were out of the eye of the storm with regard to a premature delivery. I was grateful Evan was home, and we made Christmas happen for our children.

Ironically, the due date for the baby came and went. After all of the interventions to prevent an early delivery, this new baby seemed now to be determined to not enter our world. My doctor scheduled a date for an induction. January 8th was the date chosen. It was a prophetic birthday.

January 8th is also Elvis' birthday. Yes, Elvis Aaron Presley. In 1996, January 8th fell on a Monday. We were told to report to the hospital on Sunday evening, so the very early morning induction could occur. The Christmas tree was down, we had friends and family lined up to carpool our older children to school and all of their activities, and thought we were settled.

That is when the snow began to fall.

And fall it did. Throughout the weekend, intensifying on Sunday. As we headed towards the hospital, I announced I needed eggrolls from our favorite Chinese restaurant, which was one of the only places still open in the storm. We picked up the eggrolls, and drove out on the deserted highway, each of us trying to downplay that we were one of the only cars on the road that night. It took a long time, and the eggrolls were long gone by the time we arrived at the hospital.

We settled in for a sleepless night. My doctor called, to say she was not sure she could make it to the hospital due to the snowstorm. Evan, usually even-tempered, replied in a voice that was less than polite. His response? "If we could get here, then you can, too!"

The television was playing footage of everyone who was making the pilgrimage to Graceland to mark the birthdate of The King of Rock and Roll. The headline in the paper declared we were in the midst of the, "Snowstorm of the Century!"

It is ironic, because all of these defining details are actually the perfect backdrop for the birth of my last child.

My doctor did arrive early in the morning. The induction began. Things were progressing, and it was finally time to receive the epidural.

I learned with the birth of my first daughter that I was wired to need anesthesia to get through the delivery of my babies. When Jessica was due, I made the decision to have a, "natural" delivery, and refused all offers of help with the pain of delivery. When she decided to arrive, it was near midnight, and I was doing all of the deep breathing, and relaxation techniques that I was taught in my natural childbirth classes. I thought I had it all under control. I was about to learn that I was very wrong.

At around 3am the morning of the birth of my first daughter, when the anesthesiologist came into my room to ask if I was sure I did not need any help. There was an emergency surgery that was about to take place, and she was not going to be available to me once she began that case. I was breathing...hee, hee, ha..hee, hee, ha...and assured her I was fine. It was uncomfortable, but I was good to go.

About twenty minutes after she departed, my water broke. Since it was my first time to go through the experience, I had no frame of reference. My pain went from uncomfortable to unimaginable. At one point, I opened my eyes and discovered that Gary, Jessica's father, was no longer holding my hand. He had gotten sick watching me writhe in pain, and a nurse had taken his place. I asked for help with the pain. I will never forget she told me that they had to page the anesthesiologist on call since the anesthesiologist at the hospital was now in surgery with the emergency patient. She told me that it would be about 45 minutes before the second person arrived. I remembered panicking, and saying, "THAT IS 45 MORE CONTRACTIONS!"

It was. The wave of relief that ran over me when the epidural was administered was immediate, and welcomed. Gary showed back up in the doorway, looking very pale, and uncertain. We were able to relax, and enjoy the arrival of our firstborn into the world. For the second, third, and now fourth deliveries, I was very clear that I needed that help and support.

It was quickly after the induction with baby number four that I was allowed to have the epidural. They asked Evan to step out so they could administer it. It was not too long before I realized that something was not going well.

The first attempt at the epidural was declared a fail. As was the second, third, and fourth. I was in the required position, leaning forward, over my giant belly, during full-blown contractions, all that more powerful due to the induction medication. Evan forced his way into my room to ask what was taking so long. He was told things were fine, and was escorted out.

The fifth attempt at the sedation is something I will never forget. There was a blinding stab of pain, and then the familiar relief washed over, but this time just down my right side. I was repositioned in bed, and Hannah was born just a few moments later. Afterwards, my left leg went completely numb, and stayed that way for hours and hours. I woke up late that night, after Evan had gone home, to find the anesthesiologist sitting by my bedside.

He told me he wanted to check on my status. And confess that he was the lead anesthesiologist, and had been in a battle with the hospital about the products they were ordering. He told me that they had bought a large amount of the epidural units at a discount from a new distributor, but had quickly discovered that they did not work well. He said they were rigid, and instead of flexing down the direction they needed to go, they, "bounced" off of the spinal canal, and caused all the problems I had experienced. He went on to say he had to literally force the catheters into place, which had caused me the initial lack of complete sedation, and the long term sedation of my left leg. The result for me was scarring tissue around the site, which led to numbness, as well as pain, since that day.

Before I could absorb that information, my new baby was delivered to me to nurse. Hannah was frantic, inconsolable, and I immediately knew something was amiss.

Beyond being impossible to soothe, I also immediately noticed that her eyes were crossed. Not in the way that babies eyes will sometimes cross when they are newborn. They were never not crossed. My inability to calm her, or feed her was another red flag. I had been around the block a few times in this arena. I knew instinctively that something was wrong.

I asked for help. The pediatrician on call with my practice arrived the next day. He dismissed my worries. I continued to try to calm a child who was inconsolable. I had no idea what to do. I only knew that something was very, very wrong.

We took Hannah home. I continued to regain feeling in my left leg. Evan was scheduled to leave for a company meeting a few days after we came home. He asked to be given a pass for that year's annual retreat, and was told he would be let go if he missed the meeting.

Evan was distraught to be leaving. I was distraught at the thought of him going.

There had been a lot of drama surrounding the Christmas holiday that had just passed. It sounds so silly, but it revolves around a parakeet.

Jessica had a parakeet she loved, who inexplicably died the day before Christmas Eve. We did the official send off and took her down to the local pet store to pick out a new bird. She chose a white, albino parakeet as the replacement. Her new bird was smarter, and dumber, than any of us expected.

You see, we had found that bird out of his cage a few times after successfully getting him home without incident in the sub-zero weather. His wings were clipped, so he was always walking along the carpet when we discovered him out of his cage. Repeatedly I told Jessica to secure his cage door. She was young, and I was too caught up in everything that was happening to remember to check.

At the time, we had a small dog, named "Jackson"....the best dog who was ever rescued, in the whole wide world. It would be an embarrassing, awkward conversation with one of Jessica's best friend's mother to discover that her new baby boy was the inspiration for Jackson's name!

Five days after Hannah was born, I found myself facing the inevitable. I was home, with all the children, and Evan was called away to a work meeting out of town. At the time, his boss refused to excuse him, even if it meant leaving his newborn daughter. He called my parents and asked if, on his way to the airport he could bring the older three children over so they could spend the night. They agreed, the kids were excited, and I began to get myself settled down. It was always hard to see Evan leave. This time felt like the worst. After a bout of really ugly crying, I had a better experience feeding Hannah, and she drifted off to sleep in the bassinette next to my bed. Evan had departed, the world outside was a crazy, frozen wonderland, and I was thinking I might just make it through the next several days after all.

20/20 came on the television. The house was uncharacteristically quiet. I felt myself begin to relax, muscle by muscle.

That was when Jackson appeared in the doorway of my bedroom. He was solid black, a wiry little terrier mix. Normally, I was always happy to see him. This night, I was less so.

He had tiny, bright white feathers stuck all over his snout. I only had a brief moment of confusion before my brain connected the dots.

THAT DAMN BIRD!!!!!!!!!!!!

I literally let out a scream. Hannah jolted awake and began crying at the top of her lungs. I bolted out of bed and heard myself yelling, "Drop it!"

Jackson opened his mouth, and the albino parakeet fell onto the floor. It was convulsing, and feathers continued to fall off it. I picked it up, and said, "Buddy, I know just how you feel."

I took the bird back to its' cage, and in an absurd attempt to fix things, sat it on the bottom. It promptly fell over sideways. I picked up the drape for the cage, covered it, and told myself that in the morning it would all be OK. That somehow that little bird would be standing on a perch, chirping the morning on.

I picked Hannah up. I started crying too. I called my mother, and made crazy plans to drive through the snowstorm of the century's aftermath to go to the pet store and buy another parakeet. She helped me calm down, and somehow did it without laughing at me outright.
The next few days seemed to go by in slow motion. Nothing that I ever had done for my other children worked to soothe Hannah. If anything, we seemed to be moving in the wrong direction, with her getting more upset, and frantic, with each passing hour.

My parents brought the other children home at the end of the weekend. I managed to get Hannah to drift off to sleep on Sunday afternoon, only to have her awakened by the sound of pounding in the front yard. I looked out, and saw two men, building a giant, wooden stork in the yard announcing the details for Hannah's birth. They both had on wading boots, and standing in the yard, the snow came up mid-thigh for each. I had a thought that sounds ridiculous, but scared me at the time. I thought there was a very real possibility that I might not be able to ever leave the house again. My life, as I knew it, was over. I once again began to cry.

Hard. Ugly, ugly crying, with my shoulders heaving and my nose running so hard it was flowing over my lips and dripping off my chin.

One of my children appeared in the kitchen, where I was sitting, watching the men build the stork. I was crying so hard, I could not make myself stop, or disguise it in any way. She held out a pair of jeans, and said, "When you are done crying, can you wash these for me so I can wear them tomorrow?"

I had never felt so over-my-head in all of my life until that point. Not in 1986. Not ever.

I did pull myself together to help my older children with what they needed for the school day ahead. I spent another sleepless night with a newborn who was inconsolable. I lied to Evan when he called, and told him I was fine.

I was not fine. And I knew that Hannah was not either. There was a piece missing that I simply could not solve.

It was not until Hannah's six week checkup that I began to have some sort of validation of my suspicions. I called the practice and specifically requested that Dr. Kelly see her for that appointment. He was in his late seventies, and had actually been my pediatrician. I took

Hannah in, and she was somewhat settled and calm in a pumpkin seat. Dr. Kelly walked in and said, "Let's see the new little darlin'!"

He turned the pumpkin seat around. He looked at her, and then at me, and said, "Her eyes are crossed!"

I replied, "I know! I asked about it repeatedly at the hospital. Your partners told me that all babies' eyes are crossed."

He walked across the room, picked up the phone, and made two short calls. By the next day, I was at Children's Hospital to have Hannah examined. It was the first time I had heard the term, strabismus. The muscles in her eyes were attached incorrectly, and caused the crossing. If left uncorrected, her brain would turn off the sight to her weaker eye to eliminate double vision. We were sent home with patches to alternate each day to block the vision to one of her eyes. They wanted to wait for her to gain some weight before giving her anesthesia to put her to sleep for the procedure.

The problem was, she was not gaining weight. Or sleeping. The dynamics in our family were turning upside down. We spent long periods of time to get her to slip into sleep, only to have her awaken within thirty or so minutes, with a scream that would stand your hair on end. The slightest noise would awaken her immediately. We began to impose crazy rules, like not flushing toilets at night if she were asleep, because the sound of the water running through the pipes would cause her to startle and scream. One day, Jessica emerged in the hallway, carrying her gym shoes, headed for the steps. She was on her way to school, and accidentally dropped one of her shoes. We had experienced yet another terrible night with Hannah. The sound of the shoe striking the floor caused Hannah to waken. She began screaming. So did I. Jessica began crying, and I had a point of clarity that hit me like an avalanche. We were living in an alternative reality. And every one of us was suffering.

I began to call the doctor on an almost daily basis. Our world grew smaller and smaller. Gone were the days where we could just alter our plans and head out to dinner. Any change to our routine threw Hannah into a panicked, inconsolable state of hysterics. Travelling was out of the question. Rides in the car were excruciating, with Hannah crying, as though in pain, nearly the entire time.

This went on for almost two years. The Christmas break before her second birthday everything came to a head. I had purchased new outfits for all of the children, and Hannah was no exception. She had a new, fancy dress with a tulle skirt and shiny, patent leather shoes. As Christmas break began, and we altered our schedule to accommodate the holiday festivities, she grew more and more agitated.

I had come to discover a resource in our community. A comprehensive approach to identifying developmental disorders was located in our Children's Hospital. I called, and connected with one of the intake workers. I began to explain our situation, and she told me we should get onto the waiting list. The timeline was nine months to a year, and required our pediatrician to refer Hannah there.

Christmas Day came and went and the tension in our household grew. Everyone was off school, and there was no way to get a break from what was occurring. In the middle of the break, I called the pediatrician's office, and lied. I said Hannah was running a fever and needed to be seen. My husband and I bundled her up and headed in.

As we waited for the doctor, I pulled the medical chart off the door. It was worn, and very thick. I began to page through it, and saw carbon copies of message after message where we had called for help for the past two years. Notations that

read, "Mother reports child will not eat."
"Father reports child has not slept in two days."
"Mother reports that child appears to be in
pain." "Father reports that the family needs
some direction, that they are in crisis."

Page after page, each one filled with four pink
messages. The doctor walked into the room.
She was someone we were familiar with in the
practice. She immediately expressed
displeasure at the sight of us reading Hannah's
chart, going so far as to suggest we were doing
something wrong. Evan and I shared with her
that we both were medical professionals, and
knew we had a right to the information.

She was not happy to be challenged. She shared
that Hannah no longer appeared to have a
fever. We shared that she did not have a fever
at all, we had simply said that so we could get
an appointment. Obviously calling and
reporting what was really going on was not
getting us anywhere. I expressed concern about
how far Hannah was falling behind on the
benchmarking with regard to developmental
milestones. I asked if she would provide a
referral for Hannah to get the comprehensive
evaluation at Children's Hospital. We were
incredulous when she refused, and said she
thought we were overreacting. She went so far
as to suggest that we attend parenting classes

so we could learn some tools for handling a two year old. She then told us that she would not support our decision to try to go to anyone else for a referral, and that insurance would therefore not cover any of the treatments.

We pointed out to her that Hannah was, in fact, our SIXTH child, and that we had been around the block a few times with children who are grumpy and upset. That this was far deeper, and we believed something was being totally overlooked. She dismissed our concerns, and started towards the door of the examination room. Hannah was crying. Evan and I were as well. I said, "I now understand how parents snap in the middle of the night, and hurt a child." Astonishingly, she then offered, "If you really can't take screaming tonight, you can drive to the Emergency Room at The Children's Hospital and tell them you feel you might hurt her. They will be required to keep her for at least twenty-four hours and you will get a break."

We were amazed. We shared that we were not interested in having social services take our children away. We simply wanted help.

By that point in time, Evan and I had gotten into the habit of taking turns staying up with Hannah throughout the night. When Evan was in town, he would stay up, and I would try to sleep alone in our bedroom, and on weeks like Christmas break, we alternated. The night after the disastrous visit to the doctor's office was my turn to monitor Hannah. Evan closed the door to the bedroom and fell asleep.

I soothed Hannah. She drifted off to sleep for about twenty minutes. Woke up screaming. I soothed Hannah for about thirty minutes, and she fell asleep again for about twenty minutes. Woke up screaming. The cycle continued.

This particular night, something snapped inside of me. I kept thinking of the doctor who had sent us back home and how she, and her family were likely having a peaceful night. The next time Hannah woke up screaming, I picked up our phone. It was about 2am. I called the answering service for our doctor's office. A woman answered and asked what I needed. I told her I wanted the doctor-on-call paged because my daughter was awake, and screaming, and I was unable to soothe her. She was not at all impressed. She informed me that the answering service was for true medical emergencies. I thanked her, hung up, worked to soothe Hannah, who fell into a fitful sleep. About fifteen minutes later, she woke up again, screaming hysterically. I picked up the phone, and called the answering service again. Once again, she told me, with a lot more force, that I was abusing the purpose for the line.

We continued this circle several more times. At approximately 6am, the doctor-on-call, who happened to be the nephew of the pediatrician who was my doctor, and had correctly diagnosed Hannah with strabismus, was on the other line.

His question? "What in the world is going on at your house?"

I replied, "Nothing different than any other night. Hannah is up. So am I. None of my family can actually sleep. I thought maybe whoever was on call should be awake too. I plan to do this every night going forward until somebody does something to help us."

He audibly gasped. He then said he did not realize that she was always crying. In exasperation I said, "How many times, and ways, can we say it? It is like when we asked about her eyes being crossed. She is never, ever, not crying!

He told us to go right away to the Emergency Room at Children's Hospital. Not to tell them we thought we might hurt Hannah, but to tell them we needed a full evaluation. When we got there, it was very early, and I saw the sign for the developmental delays unit across the lobby. A lesson I have learned over and over is that divine intervention and help is always looking over us. The exact intake worker who I had been talking to all along was at the desk. I recognized her nameplate, and introduced myself. She remembered me, and followed me to the ER waiting area. The staff of the ER had placed us into an isolation room to wait to be seen. Not because Hannah was contagious. Because she was so distraught, she was upsetting the other children in the larger waiting area with her crying. When I opened the door to the room to introduce the intake worker to Hannah, she was rolling across the floor, back and forth, in an almost hypnotic fashion. She was still crying uncontrollably. The intake worker stood transfixed. I asked her if she thought Hannah could benefit from being evaluated at the center for developmental disorders. After a long, pregnant pause she almost choked out, "How have you both handled this without support for this long?"

Evan and I said the same thing, almost in the same breath. What choice did we have? We did not believe in giving up, and therefore we had continued on one day at a time.

Hannah was seen by the doctor on charge, who rendered two different, life-changing opinions. One was that she should be referred to the center for developmental disorders immediately. Which meant she was being skipped ahead, and there would be no waiting period for her to be evaluated. The second was troubling for us. She was diagnosed to be in a full-blown sleep disorder. After nearly two years of asking about this prospect, and being told that it was not possible for a child that young to have such a problem, we learned there was an entire wing at The Children's Hospital that was dedicated to the treatment of children with just such a disorder.

By the time the doctor recommended that Hannah be admitted to the sleep disorders unit, Evan and I realized that she would be totally distressed by the break in her routine. We shared our concerns with the doctor. We begged to take her home with us, and watch over her as she took the medicine that he was prescribing there. He expressed grave concerns about her falling too deeply into sleep with it, and the possibility of her suffocating. The medicine she was being given was chloral hydrate. The doctor told us that Hannah was in a full-blown sleep disorder that was going to need intentional, drug-induced interruption. It took a while, but the doctor finally relented when both Evan and I produced our credentials as professionals in the medical field, and promised that one of us would remain awake, and by her crib every moment for the foreseeable future until everyone was certain that the medication was effective, and prescribed in the correct dosage.

Karma? The doctor at the ER decided he wanted the pediatrician's office to call the prescription in for the chloral hydrate. The doctor in the office that day was the very doctor who had turned us away just the day before. We were standing right next to him as he spoke with her on the phone. He questioned her. "Why are you treating these parents like this is their first baby and they have a baby with colic? This little girl has developed a sleep disorder while under your care!"

We went to the pharmacy and filled the prescription. We took Hannah home. It was late in the day, and we tentatively gave her the medicine. We placed her in her crib, and said a prayer. It was like a miracle, to see her actually relax, breathe deeply and go to sleep for the first time ever.

It was unnerving how quiet the house was. Evan and I did not take turns that night. We held our breath as we watched our daughter sleep. And experienced the peace that fell over the house. Her prescription called for four nights on, and three nights off, of the medicine. They hoped it would only take a few weeks to correct things, and she could stop taking it altogether. It took more than six months. The sleeping got better, but nothing else did, until we began to go through the evaluation process at the developmental disorders unit at Children's Hospital.

An extensive, inclusive, evaluation process encompassed every element of development. Emotional, physical, psychological, neurological, you name it, there was an expert who was assigned to evaluate that area. Divine intervention occurred again.

We were always involved in our church, and carried a deep faith. A friend of ours there happened to be an occupational therapist. She knew our family, and had watched our journey with Hannah. I shared with her that we were going through the evaluation process at Children's Hospital to try to figure out what was happening. She asked me if I had ever heard of sensory integration disorder.

I had not. She took her card out of her wallet, wrote those three words down, and told me to ask the doctors for that to be added to the things that they were screening Hannah for. It turned out to be the lynchpin for everything that was to follow.

Marcia could not have known it at the time, but her stepping forward and getting involved changed the course of our lives. Sensory integration disorder was a new diagnosis at that time, and no one really was sure what to do with it. I ran forward and turned over every stone I could to find every resource that was available to help Hannah.

Marcia became a key to unlock what was happening with Hannah. She agreed to serve as Hannah's occupational therapist and help her, and all of us with what the diagnosis meant. She told me that, in a nutshell, sensory integration disorder was an overload, of sorts, for the brain. That all of us have a degree of overload, whether it is that we cannot stand the feel of wool, or possibly silk, against our skin. The best example I was ever given was to imagine what happened when someone walked into the classroom and ran their fingernails down the chalkboard, and the resulting, hair-raising, teeth-clenching physical reaction that occurred as a result. That is what sensory overload is like. An over-exaggeration from an intake of external stimuli that is out of proportion. Hannah was experiencing that for everything that was coming into her receptors. Small noises sounded like explosions. Car seatbelts felt painful. Crinoline skirts felt too scratchy. Tags in her tee shirts were unbearable.

Everything began to make sense. And at the same time was so overwhelming.

As the evaluation process proceeded, and the Sensory Integration Disorder lens was taken into account, the final diagnosis was just that. To compound the challenges Hannah was facing was that people with this disorder rely more heavily on their visual cues. Hannah had the additional handicap of having her vision impacted by strabismus, and therefore was unable to turn to her eyesight for support. We continued to work with the new group of doctors who were helping us through this unknown pathway. Things began to improve. It was a long, arduous journey to get Hannah to the place where she needed to be in order to be successful in preschool, elementary school, and beyond. As things began to improve, we thought we had scaled the highest mountain we would ever face. We were wrong.

The lesson learned from Hannah's birth? The doctors do not always get it right. Fight for what your gut is telling you. At one point, it was suggested to us that we place Hannah in a school for special students, which was programmed for autistic children. We felt strongly that if we had enrolled her there, it would encourage autistic tendencies and do nothing to help her progress to live her fullest life. We were correct in that feeling. It helped us learn to trust in our intuition.

The next few years were ones of success and progress. We had no way to know that there were days ahead that would be one hundred fold more difficult, and tear our family ties to the point of shattering our marriage. For that, we have a few more years and no idea that we were actually in a boat on a calm stream, with an unseen rapids, and deadly drop off, just around the bend. Before that happens, however, I had to learn the lesson that to date, was the most difficult one in my life.

Chapter 12 (1999) I Cannot Save My Father

You must have been a beautiful baby. You must have been a wonderful child. When you were only starting to go to Kindergarten, I bet you drove the little boys wild. And when it came to winning blue ribbons, you must have shown the other kids how. I can see the judges' eyes as they handed you the prize. I bet you made the cutest bow. Oh, you must have been a beautiful baby, cause, baby, look at you now~You Must Have Been A Beautiful Baby, Bing Crosby

I can remember driving around town with my father. Those were happy times. He always seemed to be either whistling, or singing. He often sang, "You Must Have Been A Beautiful Baby" to me. My father was larger than life to me. He was solid, and I suppose I made the assumption that many children do, that he would always be with me.

One thing I was absolutely certain of was that my father loved me. He was loving, and kind to me. He also was very human.

My father's mother, my grandmother, died from complications of childbirth when my father was only six years old. His father was an alcoholic, and following the death of his mother, my father was shuffled from one household to another. My heart breaks when I think of what his childhood must have been like. There were stories I learned where he overheard people arguing about whose turn it was to take him in next. He spent some time living with his Boy Scout leader.

Other stories included his account of not having enough money to have his hair cut properly. I heard him share that when his teacher called him up to write on the chalkboard, he would take his left hand and place it over his hairline on his neck, so as to avoid the jokes that the children would make because his hair was cut in rudimentary lines.

At times, I marvel at the fact that he was able to grow up, and become an adult capable of loving anyone.

My parents met, and married, after each of them had experienced a failed marriage. Both of them had children. I was their first born.

My father was my cheerleader, but also very demanding. I benefitted, and also had to overcome his exacting standards. He had a tendency to overlook accomplishments and victories, and focus on any shortcoming. He was generous in his love. He also could cut me through to my very soul with the common phrase, "Kimmy, you blew it!"

To this day, I continue to quiet that statement in my own head. I clearly remember when I was paged to the phone at the factory where I worked full time after I graduated high school. It was a shirt factory, and my first husband, Gary's father, was the manager. I clocked in at 7am, and clocked out at 3pm. I then went to evening classes at my beloved NKU. At the end of the first semester, my inaugural foray into higher education, I had completed 12 hours of freshman coursework. That equated to four classes. When I answered the phone at work, my father was on the other end. His message was not that I had worked full time and successfully passed my first semester of college. His message was that I had blown it. I had narrowly missed being on the Dean's list, and therefore would not be listed in the local newspaper the way other students from our community would be. He was disappointed. I was crestfallen.

I write this to say that he was human. Actually given the tools he began with in life, he rose above the obstacles, and lived a full, blessed life. He was adored as a grandfather. I tried to ignore the fact that he was getting older. He never slowed down, so that made it easier to look the other way as the clock continued to tick. All of that changed the summer of 1999.

My father used to say that he thought the world could possibly end before the turn of the century. Sometimes, he said he could remember that his mother, who he always described as a great scholar of the bible, expressed the same sentiment. He just seemed to truly believe that everything would end before the new century could begin. It was unsettling, to say the least, to hear his thoughts on this subject.

I had successfully gotten through my Master's program of study in 1998. I then decided to pursue my Doctorate at The University of Cincinnati. The lessons I had learned from my teachers about my ability to successfully navigate the intimidating world of mathematics had paid off. I was very busy between work, school, and my family. I had not seen my mother and father as much as I would have liked. My children saw them more often, as they walked to their house from school several days a week.

1999 began routinely enough. As the winter gave way to spring, my father returned to his beloved flea market activities. He then slowed down due to getting ill with the shingles virus. He started to stay home from the flea market, which was uncharacteristic for him.

Spring turned to summer. My father did not rebound the way we expected. As summer began to end, I answered a phone call from my mother. She said, "Something just isn't right with your dad. Would you come by, and just let me know what you think?"

I walked into my parent's home, the one I had so vehemently fought moving to more than twenty years before, and sat down with my father. My medical training took over. I looked at him, and realized he had gotten smaller. Frailer. Even the ball cap he was wearing seemed too big now. My stomach knotted, and a lump rose in my throat. I allowed myself to think about the fact that I was looking at a cancer victim.

I did not communicate those thoughts to my parents at the time. I simply hugged them both, and then went home. From there, I called a trusted friend and colleague, who was a Radiologist at the hospital where my parents went for medical care. Dr. Miller assured me that he would go and collect all of the test results that were performed on my father across

163

the last few months. I cautiously shared my deepest fear with him. That my father had cancer.

Dr. Miller told me to come in with my parents the following Tuesday which was the day after Labor Day that summer. I remember I was running late. I had on green slacks, a white shirt, and was in full clinical professional mode. I was going to find the underlying cause of this!

My father was laying on a stretcher, my mother next to him when I arrived. Tim Miller made a joke, saying it was nice I had finally decided to join them. He then became very professional.

He looked at me, and said, "Well, as it turns out, you were right. He does have cancer. He had several tests this summer here at the hospital, but they were either inconclusive, or they were not communicated across the different departments. He did have shingles, on his lower back, which caused a lot of pain. However, the real problem is, he has primary site kidney cancer. We are looking at a fatality diagnosis. I'm sorry."

Time froze for me. I struggled to figure out how to react. My parents were there. I desperately wanted to be the child, and be taken care of, but understood that they needed me to take the lead. My father appeared to have not processed anything that Tim had said. My mother looked stunned. Tim shook my father's hand, and said, "I am sure I will be seeing you soon." After he walked away I said, "I can't believe it is cancer!" My father looked bewildered and I slowly began to realize that he had no way to process what he had heard at that time.

I left, determined to find some way to turn everything around. My world simply did not work without my father in it.

I was working a full time faculty position at The University of Cincinnati. I was also taking full time classes as a doctoral student. I had four children, two step-children, and a husband in the mix. I began to panic that I was running out of time. At this point, my father was home much more than he was out and about. I went to visit one night, not long after Tim's revelation.

My mother was there and we were enjoying a good time together. I had recently taken a new position, as an assistant professor at The University of Cincinnati. My father asked for my business card. I handed it to him, and he got emotional. He looked at my mother and said, "Jean, did you ever think we would see something like this?"

I then announced the decision I had arrived at. I told my father that I was going to take a break from my student work. I had so many evening classes. I just thought I needed to have more time to come over to spend with them.

I will never forget what he said next. "What in the hell are you planning to do? Just come over every night and stare at me? I want you to make me a promise. I want you to stay in school. I am going to be fine. Do not quit. Promise me that you will not quit school."

I did not quit after that. I did a lot of soul-searching and realized that, even if I went over every single evening, there really was not anything left for me to say to my father. I loved him. He knew that.

One of the most difficult days that happened going forward was visiting on Halloween. We had a long-standing tradition of going first to trick or treat with the children to their home. My mother had pulled a chair out onto the porch for my father to sit in. He was in good spirits. The ball cap looked like it was wearing him instead of the other way around. I stopped midway up between the car and the porch. I no longer could pretend that my father was going to get well.

His disease was rapid, and in hindsight, was merciful to our family. He had a very difficult time accepting his diagnosis at first. He did not want to talk about it. At one point, I asked if I could tape his responses to the stories he knew so well. He was actually a living historian to the region, and what had transpired there during the course of his life. At the time, he scolded me, and said, "What do you think? Do you think I am going to die?!"

By the time he had come to acceptance about his medical condition he was too weak to have me do any sort of oral history. He offered to do the oral history at that time, but there was no way to get that accomplished as he was failing daily. His stories are ones I now write down, but his voice lives on only in my memory.

On December 15th, my father was transferred to the hospice unit of our local hospital. It was a cold night. He had fallen into a coma and was totally unresponsive. We wanted him to be as comfortable as possible, and made the decision to transfer him to the hospice unit so they could care for him through to the time of death. My younger sister's former boyfriend of many years had chosen that night to come and visit. He had been close for many years with our family, and had learned that our father was very sick. He was carrying a large poinsettia.

Matt arrived, and everything else began to happen quickly. The ambulance showed up. The EMT workers struggled to place him onto the carrier they provided. Finally, the men carried my father out of the door. I delayed a bit in following them. I took Matt's flowers into the house, and then began to cry. I remember saying that I knew my father would never, ever, be coming home. I cried, and cried and cried. Matt just stood in silence, held me, and helped me through that difficult time.

I drove to the hospital. My father was in a comatose state. He had finally acknowledged that he was at the end of his life, and was then medicated as such to alleviate his pain. He was settled into his bed. I found myself alone for a few minutes with him. I took his hand, and in what I know was his last message to me, he opened his eyes. He squeezed my hand, and his eyes grew clearer. It was just for a moment. He was on so much pain medication that it had an unsettling effect of causing his eyes to not always be aligned. For this last exchange, he looked straight at me, and smiled. Words were not needed. Then, as quickly as he had awoken, he slipped back into a deep sleep.

The doctors told us that they expected it to be about three or four days until death occurred. I went home. My mother spent a long time with him, and then she eventually went back to her home. The next morning was a Thursday. I was getting ready to go to the university to work when I received a call from my mother. They were calling the family in. They now believed it would be a matter of hours, instead of days.

My mother told me that when she returned to his room, there was a minister waiting. In the time it took her to make three phone calls, my father had passed away. The hospice workers are some of God's most special people. One of them later told me that they often see people pass quickly, when they are able to let go, and transition. It occurred to me that until we had transferred my father to the hospice unit, family members had surrounded him, and it was probably very difficult for him to turn loose of this life.

I did not know that he had died when I arrived at the hospital with Evan. I walked into the room, and saw the very big difference in the energy from the evening before. It had really only been a few hours since I was sitting there next to my father for that last meaningful gaze. The body lying on the bed now looked so empty, so devoid of his spirit. I felt my knees begin to

169

buckle. I made it to the side of the room, where a large trash can was sitting on the floor. I began to wretch, and thought my very soul was going to be ripped from my being.

The staff at the hospital were wonderful to us. As the day progressed I realized we had children who were at school, and had no idea that their grandfather was now gone. Our youngest, Hannah, was just a month away from her fourth birthday, and was not able to comprehend the gravity of the past few weeks and months.

We began to make plans. Our family came together and we helped one another through this most difficult time. We chose to have the visitation on the next Sunday evening, and then the funeral on the Monday morning after. The funeral home was decorated for Christmas, and Christmas carols were playing softly on the overhead speakers. It would be years, and years before I would ever be able to enjoy Christmas music again.

My children handled this loss in their own individual ways. Hannah, who always had her security blanket with her to sleep, ran up the stairs to my father's bedroom the first time we went back to the house after his death. I suddenly realized that she was heading up to say hello to her grandfather. She arrived at the top of the stairs looking very confused. She looked down at us and asked, "Where are grandpa's blankies?" We all began to cry.

Our son was only in second grade. He wrote a beautiful letter about his grandfather, that I still have to this day.

The older girls were quiet. They seemed mostly concerned about how upset I was. I simply could not stop crying. The morning when he died at that hospital, I remember how surreal it felt to be on the elevator riding down to the front door, and that everyone around me was going on as if the world had not just ended.

We had wonderful support from family and friends. The day of the funeral, I remember saying over and over that I didn't know what to do. A friend grabbed my hands, and said, "You don't have to know what to do right now." Everyone kept assuring me things would eventually be alright. I was not so sure.

When it was time to go to the graveyard, I had the most unreasonable thought process happening. It was a cold, bitter day outside. I kept thinking it was the worst thing to leave my father outside in the freezing cold that way. Since he was a veteran, there was a twenty-one gun salute offered. Each ricochet of the sounds of the gunshots felt as if they were going through my heart.

Time does help. But what I learned from this chapter in my life is that the loss is never fully absorbed. Every milestone achieved is a bit lessened because he is not here. One evening, my son called me, so excited, from the top of the stairs. As was our routine, he had been put to bed with a book to read. He walked back into his room, and looked upset. He then told me that he had been reading his book to his grandpa. That he was sitting with him until I came up the stairs.

It was a long while before I experienced the presence of my father after his death. One summer, we went to the beach for a vacation. Long after everyone was in bed, I walked outside and climbed into the lifeguard's big, wooden chair. I stared out into the dark, listening to the waves crash against the shore. I cried, and yelled, "Where are you? Where are you?!" Staring up into the dark, night sky, I wondered what his journey had been like as he transitioned out of this world.

It was quite a long time before I finally began to see my father. A counselor at the hospice center told me that it could take longer for me to be able to be receptive and see signs of his presence since the wound was so raw, and the pain was so deep. One day, I woke up. Woke fully up, not in a state of dreaming. My father was there, in his familiar ball cap. He told me that things were going to be OK. A peace surrounded me for the first time since he passed. It was close to the time that I was about to graduate with my doctorate. It would prove to be the first ceremony that I had where my father was not present in the physical sense. I crossed that stage, and knew that I had kept my promise to my father. I had not quit. He was with me.

Several years later, after the descent into darkness began with my son, I would see my father again. We were at the high school, for the opening night of "Godspell." Ej was the first person on the stage, singing, "Prepare Ye The Way Of The Lord." Ironically, it was the same play that I watched Leo perform all those years ago when I was a freshman in high school. I had allowed myself to celebrate that night, because, we were watching our son being torn away from us, but thought maybe this was a new, positive, direction. For the opening night of Godspell, things seemed to normalize, and I was cautiously hopeful that we were not going to lose him after all. At the end of the show, the cast came out and took their bows. I looked across the auditorium, and saw a familiar face. Actually, it wasn't his face, but the back of his head. I saw who I knew to be my father pushing open the side door to exit, with the same familiar coat, and ballcap, silver hair showing beneath it. Just as I thought I must be imagining it, I looked at the stage and saw Ej, transfixed, looking at him too. Ej looked at me. Our eyes locked. We both knew that his grandpa had made it to the opening night of his show.

Chapter 13 (2004) Going Home to NKU and the Descent into Darkness

Hello. Is there anybody out there? Just nod if you can hear me. Is there anyone at home? Come on now, I hear you're feeling down. I can ease your pain. And get you on your feet again. Relax. I'll need some information, first. Just the basic facts. Can you show me where it hurts? There is no pain you are receding. A distant ship smoke on the horizon. You are only coming through in waves. Your lips move but I can't hear what you're saying. When I was a child I had a fever. My hands felt just like two balloons. Now I've got that feeling once again. I can't explain you would not understand.~Comfortably Numb, Pink Floyd

2004 was a year that was a study in contrasts. In so many ways it was a year of positive beginnings. In so many others, it was a terrible foreboding of endings that would be so painful.

2004 was the year that my oldest daughter graduated from high school. All at once I realized I was out of time. Completely, totally, out of time. Jessica was on her way to college.

Which meant she was on her way to moving out of our home. I was not handling that very well.

She also was in love. Completely, hopelessly, head over heels in love. Again, there would be a life pattern that was being repeated. She was in love with her high school sweetheart. A boy she described as someone she could not even imagine dating a few years before. Kevin was the star of the high school in every way. He was a year ahead of her, and it reminded me so much of how Leo dominated my high school so many years before. They found themselves in a high school play, and the day came when Jessica told me that she had been asked out by Kevin.

We were entering the Christmas season of 2002 at that point. There was an activity that was on the horizon, for the students who were participating in reenacting the Victorian Christmas activities. As it turned out, there were not any costumes left that Jessica could access. I stepped in, and rented her a beautiful period gown from a local costume shop. It was green, and complimented her red hair and fair skin so well. She was paired with Kevin for the first dance in the program. I took a picture, as she bowed, and Kevin took her hand. It turned out to be a prophetic photograph.

Less than a week later, Jessica and Sara both were performing in our church's Christmas cantata. They both were pirouetting up the aisle of the church in the final Halleluiah chorus. Kevin had asked to come. He was sitting on my right. My husband, Evan was sitting on my left. As Jessica came up the aisle, Kevin took ahold of the back of the pew right in front of us. I remember looking at him. And then I said, "Oh no." I had seen that look before. They were so young. And yet, I knew, it was already something that was set in motion that I had no vote in. Kevin was in love with her. It was obvious.

At this point, I was working in the corporate arena, and hours were long. Evan was still travelling, but the children had gotten much older, and it was easier for me to juggle things. I had graduated with my doctorate in 2002, so my classwork was behind me. Hannah continued to grow and develop, and I thought we had turned a major corner in life. But as it often occurs, there was a bigger mountain just over the horizon.

As Jessica neared her high school graduation, Sara began to worry us a great deal. She was sick, but no one seemed to understand what was happening. It would ebb and flow, and since she was a very dedicated student, she often pushed herself and did not tell us when she was not feeling well. Instead, she went to school.

I experienced a flood of emotions as Jessica graduated, and then excitedly made plans to move away to go to college. I was proud of her, of course. Proud of us, actually. I thought back more than once to the terrible day when I realized that she and I, and her sister, soon to be born, were on our own, and had no idea how we would move forward. We had made it. Her high school diploma proved that we had succeeded. It really did take a village, with family, friends, and, ultimately, Evan, coming into our lives to get us across the finish line.

Sara continued to lose weight. During the first week of her senior year of high school, we received a call. She had fainted and was in the nurse's office. Evan rushed up and brought her home, and then called me at work. Visibly shaken, he reported that she was so weak she was having trouble walking. She was so thin, he could actually carry her. We continued to push the doctors, who continued to miss the mark, and, at one point, suggested to me that we were overlooking either an eating disorder, or even a drug issue. I knew that was not the case. Deep in my gut, I knew that something was drastically wrong.

Right about that time, our son, Ej, was experiencing problems that we had never expected. He was moody, and upset, and acting out in ways that were cruel, and completely unlike him. I began to ask the doctors if perhaps there was something going on with him that might involve an eating disorder, or worse. He had gained weight, before he had gotten taller, and was bullied for it. Within a dramatically short amount of time, he was quite thin. I again had the terrible feeling deep in my gut, and knew something was dreadfully wrong. The foreboding I felt was palpable.

A second time, Sara fainted and Evan picked her up. It was then that I learned that near the end of her Junior year, while Jessica was still there, this was a common occurrence, but that Sara, not wanting to miss school, had a system worked out. If she was sick, or fainted, her or Jessica's friends connected the two of them and Jessica helped her to class so she did not have to go home sick. Now that Jessica was in college, and many of their common friends had graduated with her the spring before, it was coming more to the attention of the teachers, who delivered her to the nurse, who then called us.

That particular day, I was working at a freestanding medical imaging facility. I was close to the owner of the company, and rushed to his office, as he was a doctor. I interrupted him as he was speaking with a Nuclear Medicine technologist. I literally burst in and began explaining Sara's symptoms, and begged him to write an order to have Sara scanned from head to toe. I heard myself saying, "She is dying right in front of us, and no one seems to know what to do!"

God stepped in.

The tech in the office, who I did not know well, quietly said, "That sounds like Grave's disease."

What? In all of my years in the medical field, I had not heard of this particular disorder. I did not know anyone who had it. I questioned her at length, and then rushed off to call Sara's pediatrician. It was the same doctor on call that day who had written the order to allow us to take Hannah to the emergency room years before. He came to the phone, and hands shaking, I said, "Kevin, could it be Grave's disease?"

There was a long, pregnant pause. When he began to speak his voice filled with panic. He told me to go right away, pick Sara up, and go straight to Children's Hospital. He called the medical director of the unit that handles hormonal dysfunction and disease. Graves disease causes the thyroid gland to work overtime. It causes the body to be in a constant state of hyperactive performance, as though one were running a marathon at all times. If you stress the body, by doing something like climbing the staircase at the high school, the additional stress on the heart causes the body to shut down in a fainting spell. There simply is not a way to handle getting the blood circulated to the brain. It stresses the heart, and causes the patient to feel overheated at all times.

The reason it was overlooked for so long is because the disease usually has an onset in midlife. I learned that it is something that can strike a child. Sara was surrounded with other pediatric patients at the hospital. The director told us that, in her practice, Sara was arguably one of the sickest patients she had ever encountered, and that she estimated that we were only weeks away from a catastrophic heart event as the overtaxing became lethal. I was without words, but so grateful that we finally had an answer. Our attention turned to Sara and she fought back for months to get onto solid ground. It is a miracle that she is here, and I will always know that the tech, that God placed in my pathway that fateful day, is the reason we finally found an answer.

Several months passed. I received a wonderful professional opportunity. My undergraduate alma mater had a position posted that I learned about and began to pursue. It was to serve as the right hand of the president there. It was not something that I would have ever considered could happen way back when I first showed up at the campus on shaky knees as a first-generation college student. But step by step, the process continued to unfold, and in October of that year I was named to the role. I marveled many times throughout my tenure there that I could go into a building, such as the library, close my eyes, and literally travel back into my memories so it felt like my first days there. The sights, sounds, and even smells there could trigger a powerful emotional reaction. I felt blessed, and lucky, and also resolved to work to the utmost of my ability to earn the respect of those who had placed me into that opportunity.

There was a wonderful entry period to my new job. I began work on a Friday, October 1st to be exact. The president asked me if I could travel to New York City on Saturday, October 2nd to assist him as he was ascending to the presidency of a national organization. I jokingly began to refer to him as the president squared. He was gracious, and kind, and placed me into a well-oiled machine that allowed me to learn.

We went to New York. The conference was held in lower Manhattan, just blocks away from ground zero. When we arrived, we met with his colleagues, and walked to a deli, bought sandwiches, and sat in Battery Park to eat. We then walked the perimeter of the site of the former World Trade Center buildings. It was an amazing experience for me. I had never seen New York before, and never expected to be standing on that hallowed ground.

Later, we all headed back to the hotel. I went to my room, grateful for the break in the action. I was not in my room long when the phone rang. It was my new boss.

He said, "Hello Kimberly! This is Jim. Jim Votruba." I remember thinking that I knew who he was without his last name!

He then went on, "Do you have any plans tonight? Because if you don't, I have plans for you. The Executive Committee is going to dinner, and then to a show on Broadway. Rachel (his spouse who I so admired) didn't come this trip so there is an extra ticket. If you don't have any plans, would you like to join the group?"

The rest of the night was simply magical for me. Orchestrated down to the last tiny thing. I went to the elevator a short time later, and when it stopped on my floor, the doors opened, and there stood my new boss. The group of people that we met in the lobby were just wonderful. I was accepted with open arms. We ate at Sardi's Restaurant, where I wandered around looking at the artwork on the wall, and thinking about how many movie scenes I had watched that had been filmed there.

Afterwards, we walked a short distance to The James Theater. We were about to take in *The Producers.* As we walked, Jim leaned down, and whispered, "Stop looking up at the buildings!"

He was amused. I had not realized it until that point, but I was literally walking along, slack-jawed, looking up at all the buildings along the skyline. The group of people we were with were very kind to me, and I was struck by how much I could relate to them. It was the beginning of my foray into the C-Suite level, and finding myself comfortable to be there.

The opening of the play was a bit raunchy, and at one point, an obscenity was screamed that was really quite funny. I froze, because I was sitting between two university presidents, and the seats were so close our knees were practically touching. My first reaction was to laugh, but I was unsure what was politically correct in my new environment. I did not have to wait too long.

Both presidents burst out into laughter. I did as well. The realization that they were equally professional, deeply approachable and human was wonderful. Once the play reached the intermission, it was easily 10pm. At that point, my day had reached its' 15th hour. Jim looked at me and said, "How are you holding up?" I heard myself respond, "I'm great! Do you know we are on Broadway!!!"

After the show, the cabs were very scarce. We were waiting with another couple and returning to the same hotel. One lonely cab emerged from the shadows, and we asked if he could take all of us. He agreed. Jim walked up to the front door on the passenger side, and began to open the door. The cab driver immediately said that was against the rules, and that all four of us would have to sit in the small back seat. We looked at one another, and decided pretty quickly that was exactly what we would do. We squeezed in, and every time we rounded a corner I fell into the person's lap on that side. It was a really fun night, and it forged lifelong friendships that I will forever cherish.

As the academic year continued, Jessica decided she was not content with the college she had chosen. She came home for Christmas, and took a three week class, and fell in love with Northern Kentucky University the way I had decades before. She made the decision to finish the academic year, and then transfer for good to NKU. Sara continued to improve, and Hannah was progressing well under the care of a wonderful group of teachers, spearheaded by Mrs. Dennis, who handled all of her special needs.

Ej was not doing as well. I sat at my desk one afternoon, and wrote a heart wrenching email to the principal of his school. It began, "I am so concerned about my son."

It went on to detail the behavioral changes. The anger, and obstinacy. We had caught him lying, and being cruel to others, which was a total departure of the child that we had known. I described the physical changes, including the drastic loss of weight, and the refusal to eat. I pled for help and intercession.

We also turned to our doctor. We asked if there was an eating disorder that was happening.

What about mental health issues? Could there be an underlying drug issue?

We did not receive any answers. It was a long time before the gravity of what was happening came to light.

Sara graduated high school, and went to live in the dorms of Northern Kentucky University at the end of the summer. Now we were down to just Hannah and Ej living at home. Things were about to get so much darker. It would prove to be a darkness that would descend, and a storm that would obliterate everything in its' pathway before light broke back through the clouds.

Ej's behavior continued to deteriorate. Addictive behaviors began to surface. We were desperate for answers, but could not find any. Grades began to plummet, and before we knew it, violence began to be a regular part of our daily lives. The son we knew had disappeared, and it was clear to me that he was in as much pain as we were. I have never, before or since, felt so powerless as a mother.

The descent was gradual, and yet very quick, looking back. We became normalized to the lifestyle that we were leading, which included regular visits to our home by the police, and constant calls from both the school system and the police alike. Our home had turned into a war zone. Evan and I were not on the same page as to how to respond. I was trying to hold a hard line, insisting that we would not yield to what was happening. Evan was more lenient, thinking I was making everything worse. We began to do what I never thought could happen. We began to permanently drift apart.

I became so angry at the tidal wave that had taken over our lives. I began to resist going to church. I was more angry at God than anyone else. None of it made any sense to me. At all.

It was not that Evan and I had escaped the problems that marriages face across the years. Combining two families from the inception of our union was fraught with stress and complications. Money was always tight as we worked to meet the needs of all of our children. The craziness of the busy schedule of our lives did not help. Some of it we contributed to. Some of it happened to us. I grew more and more isolated. I retreated to my own space, which was one of true loneliness. Anger swallowed me completely as I watched everything that I loved slipping away.

A few years passed, and things worsened. Some of this portion of my life is almost beyond my ability to recall, because I was walking around in a place that was so frightening I could not even face it. One of the days, that should have been the happiest in my life, became the catalyst that changed everything.

Jessica and Kevin wed during the Christmas break of her senior year of college. At that point, I was struggling so hard to put on a normal face for everyone that it took all the energy that I had. She planned the perfect Christmas wedding, which brought back all of my hopes and dreams of my wedding to her birth father years before. As I watched her and Kevin, so in love, and so happy, I felt more isolated than ever from Evan. By that point we rarely spoke, and were living essentially estranged lives in the battle zone of our home. The wedding was beautiful. I cried myself to sleep that night, not because I felt I had lost my daughter. I felt I had lost myself.

Health problems descended on me that winter, leading to a cervical fusion surgery. I asked Jessica to take me to the hospital for the surgery, because Evan and I were so estranged I did not feel comfortable with him near me. I took time off work, returning just in time to see Jessica cross the stage for graduation.

I was sitting in my seat on the platform, behind the president, thinking about the first time I had crossed the stage, pregnant with Jessica so many years ago. She was a second-generation college graduate. It was such a meaningful time.

Ej was not having a good day. At that point, in time, he was not having many good days. He had been in and out of the court system, and spent some time in juvenile prison because of his drug addiction and problematic behavior. He acted out at the graduation ceremony, and by the time we got home, he was in a full-blown rage. My mother had offered to have Jessica's party at her house, alleviating me from that work, since I was still recovering. I was happy to accept. We stopped by our home to let the dogs out and regroup, and get Ej settled down. He did not.

He did not want to go to the party. We could not leave him alone. He got louder, and louder, and invariably violent. He screamed unthinkable things, and before long, the police were called yet again to our home. They were there for a while, offered no help as had become the pattern, only to say we had to figure out what to do.

I was shaken, and sick, and feeling very weak. I walked into Hannah's room, and shut the door. I said, "I am sorry the police were here again." Then, a pivotal life moment happened. She turned to me, a soul much older than her chronological age of 12, and her eyes turned flat, almost anaesthetized. She said, in a very matter-of-fact manner, "It's OK mom. I'm used to it."

My stomach did a cartwheel. My heart dropped. I felt physically sick. I then realized with sudden, terrifying clarity that Hannah had been normalized to this violent, chaotic world order that was now our life.

After more argument, we finally got everyone into the car and headed over to my mother's house for the graduation party. We walked in, very late. My mother had no way to know what had transpired. She walked up to me and said, "What took you so long? Everyone is waiting to eat!"

I began to cry. It actually was a deep, gut-wrenching sobbing that I could not stop. I went into her bedroom, and the longer I cried, the worse it got. It took everything I had to stop, and walk back out into the family room, eyes swollen, and chest hurting, simply heartbroken. I knew what I had to do.

Several months earlier, I had visited a few places I found for rent, having arrived at the decision that if, nothing was going to change, then I was going to move out, and take Hannah away from all of the chaos. It had truly become a dangerous environment. More than one of the people we sought guidance from said it had all the makings of something that could turn fatal.

One of the places I visited was a condominium for sale just about a mile away from our home. It was in the same school district, so Hannah could continue uninterrupted, which I thought was very important. It was again divine intervention that as the realtor took me through the property, I encountered the owner of the development. We spoke for a few minutes and he offered me his card. I tucked it into my wallet, and nearly six months later pulled it out the day of Jessica's graduation. I sent an email to the address listed.

I had no capacity to purchase the condominium, but I was drawn to it just the same. I left a message to ask if any of the units were still available because I had not seen the for-sale signs in the yard any longer. Almost immediately, my phone rang.

I began, "You probably don't remember me, but…"

He replied, "Red hair, right?"

I was stunned. I said, yes, I had red hair. He went on to explain, "My father and I own the complex. We were just speaking about it this week, and took the for-sale sign out of the yard after the last unit has sat for months with no offer. We just this week made the decision to lease just that last unit. In fact, if you want it, you could even choose the colors to finish it. I could meet you there tomorrow if you like."

The next day was Mother's Day. It was not like the happy ones in the years gone by. When things in my life made sense, and my children were young, Evan would arrive at the top of the stairs on that holiday and serve me breakfast in bed. Church would follow, along with darling, hand-made gifts from the children. We then would visit my mother and spend time with her. However, I no longer knew that world.

Instead, in 2008, I spent the afternoon with the man who would shortly become my property owner. He asked for a deposit to hold the unit, and told me it would be ready in about six to eight weeks. I wrote out the check, and made my way to my car. I drove up Tremont Avenue, deciding I should take a long route home, in order to give myself time to allow my hands to stop shaking. I knew that I had just redefined the entire course of my life. It felt empowering, and I was sad through to my very soul. I had just

193

taken the reins back to drive my own life forward, but in doing so, was walking away from everything I had tried to build for twenty years.

The lesson learned from that experience is that sometimes you have to do the hardest thing you have ever done, if you are to find any hope of moving forward. I presented a brave face to the world as I communicated my intentions. I secretly hoped that a miracle would happen. That things would straighten out in my home life to the point as to convince me that I should cancel the lease, and just pay the penalty and stay in the home I had built with Evan.

No such miracle happened. As the summer wound down, I booked the movers, and had a flash back to 1986, and the time when I had to leave Gary, and all of the hopes and dreams I had shared with him. That year was scarier, because I was unsure if I had what it took to make it on my own. This time was more heartbreaking, with so much more time invested, and the completely unchartered waters that lay in front of me. I did not want to leave Evan.

I would soon discover that moving around the corner would not be far enough to effect the change that needed to happen.

Chapter 14 (2010) Moving to Four States in Five Years

Take one last look before you leave, 'Cause oh, somehow it means so much to me. And if you'll ever need me, you know where I'll be. So, please, call home if ya change your mind. Oh, I don't mind. I guess I saw it comin' day by day. But, oh, I could not stand the failure. Before you leave, there's just one thing I must say, Please, call home if ya change your mind. Oh, I don't mind. And I know, you're used to runnin'. Oh, you're lost baby, and I ain't funnin'. But, oh, when you call to me, well, I'll come running'. Straight to your side, again I'll confide in you. So, go on, I won't say no more. My heart ain't in it, but I'll hold the door. But, just remember what I said before. Please, call home if ya change your mind. Please, call home if ya change your mind. Oh yeah, call home if ya change your mind. Call home if ya change your mind, oh. Please call home if ya change your mind. Oh yeah, call home baby~Please Call Home, Gregg L. Allman

As I settled into my new condominium, I felt a sense of accomplishment. Hannah and I now had a place to live free from police visits, and threats of physical harm each night as we lay down to sleep. I also was incredibly sad. I was lonely, and confused, and had no idea how I had arrived at the crossroads where I was standing.

My family was not wholly supportive. Much of it was because many of them did not understand the full scope of the issues at the house I had shared with Evan each day. I felt a sense of shame, and defeat in the fact that I had been unable to change the direction of the downward spiral. I secretly prayed, and truly believed, that I would get a call, and Evan would tell me that everything was getting better somehow, and ask me to come back. A phone call came, but it was not the message I had hoped to hear.

I was sitting in a meeting of the governing board at my work, right next to the president. Board meetings were among the most crucial events that I managed in my portfolio. My cell phone vibrated, and I glanced at the number, but did not recognize it, so ignored it.

It rang again. And again. And again.

I finally did something I never do. I stepped out of the meeting and called the number back. It was the bank who held the mortgage on the house I had moved out of several months before. They told me that they needed to alert me to the fact that my home was in the initial stages of foreclosure, and they had been unable to reach me. My name was on the mortgage along with Evan's. They had been sending the notices via mail, but I was not at the house to receive them, and they did not have any forwarding address for me. I asked how badly the payments had fallen in arears. The number they quoted stunned me. I knew at that moment that our home had just been lost, because I had no ability to close that gap.

I stood in the hallway, unable to breathe. I knew I needed to return to the board meeting. I struggled to stop my heart from racing. I forced myself to inhale. I walked back into the meeting, and to this day have no idea how I got through the rest of that day.

When I finally was able to leave for the day, I went home, and waited for Evan to bring Hannah over. I sent him a message, asking him to come in with her. When he did, I asked about the house. He looked like someone had kicked him in the stomach. He began to tell me the honest truth. He had been downsized, and fallen behind on the mortgage as he searched for work. He had hoped to get funds together to get back on track, but he had not been able to. He looked deeply ashamed, and I began to cry as the reality of what was happening truly resonated with me. The house we had made our home for nearly 16 years was lost to us. I started to think about the names of the color of paint we had picked out for the rooms. Periwinkle. Slate. Jade. I thought about the four angels I had stenciled in the laundry room, with the names and birthdates of the babies born to me. The fact that our first dog was buried in the back yard. Crying turned to uncontrollable sobbing. I knew this was the true end.

Evan turned to go. It would be years before I understood just how crippled he was by all that had happened to us. He shared, much later, his thoughts of just sitting in his car, and letting it run in the garage, and slipping into a sleep that would never end.

By the next day, I had flown into action to mitigate the financial damage to us as much as possible. I called the realtor that had helped us buy that home, and explained what had happened. She dropped all that she was doing, and placed a for sale sign in the front yard. Against all odds, in the middle of the recession of 2008, a contract came in. It was December when we closed. The couple that purchased our home was very unfriendly. As we struggled to move things out in the middle of a snowstorm, they began to threaten to come in and take everything out to the curb. I stood and watched professional piano movers take the piano that I loved out onto the slick driveway and struggle to not drop it off of the ramp as they loaded it on the truck. Hannah's basketball hoop was frozen to the ground. When it was all said and done, I simply asked my family to come over to help clean everything out. The last time I stood in the house I was totally alone. It was empty, and I was broken. I told myself that I would be able to move ahead in my life, and find happiness and financial security again. I was so angry at Evan. At God. At myself. At the universe.

I initiated divorce proceedings. It did not take long before I was officially single again.

As time went along, I became totally estranged from Ej. He moved with Evan to a rental property. Hannah bounced back and forth between our two homes. I began to realize that she was not doing well at all with the new world order. She was becoming more isolated as she headed through middle school. The day she came home with a note that she had found slipped into her locker, that proclaimed her a freak and suggested that she kill herself, I knew I had to make another, more drastic move.

My role at NKU was in its' sixth year. The president I worked for was beginning to talk about retiring. Oftentimes, the role I held did not survive the turnover of the presidency, so I was keenly aware that I might be facing a job displacement in the near future. I had been looking for opportunities, but once Hannah brought that horrible note home, I made the decision to make a geographical move, and take her with me. A fresh start for both of us.

Evan was not happy about the prospect of being separated from Hannah. We talked. He did understand that it would be in her best interest to give her a new beginning. To go someplace she would not have her family history known, and used to bully her.

I began applying, and came close to opportunities in places like Seattle, and Nashville. That fall, I received an offer from a university in West Virginia, and accepted what was essentially the same role, working directly for the president there. The only difference was I had responsibility for taking the government relations lead at the state and federal level.   It was about a 7-hour drive from home, in a secluded, beautiful part of the state. It seemed perfect.

I began my new role in mid-November. I got there, and realized right away that the home I had rented was wildly different than the one portrayed in the pictures on the internet. I pulled into the drive on a cold, wild, rainy November night. I was driving; thinking how ironic it was that it was just a few days before my anniversary, and how many miles were between Evan and me. To be truthful, I was frightened. I had never moved away from home before, and never in a million years expected to be moving away by myself. Even when I moved around the corner in Fort Thomas, everything was just harder. There was no one there to help me with even the simplest of tasks. Evan and I had always made a great team, and I missed his steady hand very much. The house before me was filthy. I walked in and saw that the banister was falling down and that the locks on the windowsills had rotted off, leaving no way to secure the premises. The back door had no lock at all, so it blew open every time the wind picked up. The deck had totally fallen off the house, so if you stepped out of the back door, you could easily fall two stories to the yard below.

I called the property owner and expressed my concerns. He showed up shortly afterwards, and I was astonished to see him walk through the house, and use a hammer to nail each windowpane so there was no possibility of opening it. I asked what I would do if I needed to get out emergently. Alternatively, open them in the summer. He laughed, and said, "There aren't any screens in the windows, so you won't want to open them anyway because the stink bugs will come in."

He left, and I began to unload my van in the freezing rain. I made trip after trip into the house with clothes, and small furniture, and the necessities I needed. At one point, I walked outside, in the sub-zero weather, to find a man standing at my van, bare foot, and wearing only shorts. He had tattoos covering a lot of him. He seemed a little scary to me. He then told me that he was my next-door neighbor. That, in fact, we shared a driveway. He then proceeded to ask me at length if I was there all alone. I grew more, and more uneasy.

I inflated an air mattress that my older sister had given me. I laid down in the upstairs bedroom, and wondered again how I had gotten where I was. How this all had happened. I began to hear a scary noise. Whoosh! Smack! Whoosh! Smack!

I cautiously followed it, and found that in the next bedroom, there was such a breeze through the nailed-shut window that the bamboo shade that hung over it was literally blowing in the wind. It would blow out, "whoosh" and then crash back against the window pane, "smack"........

Uneasy, I got up and went downstairs to get a drink of water. I opened the refrigerator door, and the light flooded in around me in the darkness. It must have been about 3am. I had two nasty surprises in store for me in the minutes that followed.

I noticed that the drawers in the refrigerator were dark. I opened one. Nasty, dirty water spilled all over the floor and my feet. There was the source of the nasty smell in the kitchen!

I felt that crazy instinct that you have when you are being watched. I glanced to my left, at the window that only had a valance. I was still outlined in the pale light of the refrigerator glow. The light in my new neighbor's window was on. There stood the man who had been relentlessly questioning me, nose pressed against his window, staring at me. I froze.

When I was able to move, I quickly shut the door. I stumbled through the darkness back up to my air mattress on the second floor. I lay there thinking about his offer to allow me to use the shared driveway that our houses used. He said he had filled in his garage with brick where the windows used to be, and no longer used it as a garage.

I could not suppress the phrase that was repeating itself in my head. It was a line from, "The Silence of the Lambs." "It puts the lotion on its' skin, or else it gets the hose again!"

I had seen that movie years before. I knew how things ended for women who were taken to the lower level of houses where the windows had been replaced by cinder blocks.

I managed to take a shower and go to work the following day. I told my coworkers that I would be moving out of that house that very day. I went back at the end of the workday, and, in reverse, made trip after trip to put everything back into my van. I then drove to the Marriott, and unloaded what I could there, and spent the next two weeks driving around with all the small furniture in tow! For anyone who can remember the Clampetts from The Beverly Hillbillies, well, that is close to how I felt each time I drove to a meeting and saw the stares at my van, complete with bar stools, and a small table inside. I was humiliated. Not so long before, that table and stools had been in the home I had shared with Evan.

As Thanksgiving approached, I began to truly appreciate how difficult it was to find any housing in that small town. There simply was nothing to be found. The Sunday before Thanksgiving arrived dreary, and rainy. I laid in bed until I could not stand it any longer. I showered, went to the van, and told myself that something needed to change that day. I prayed. I asked for help. As I drove through the town I came upon an unusual open house sign in the yard of a house. I parked, and ventured in. The realtor told me that the couple in that house needed a three-month window to vacate the house. She then listened to my story. She was empathetic, and said she thought I needed to talk to the owner of a house, that she claimed was new. That owner was a woman, and she was developing new houses just down the road, which I had not seen in my time there. She shared that there was a home, that was built in the new development, that was standing empty.

I was not sure what to think. I followed her instructions and drove right up Duck Creek Road, which transitioned into a gravel road, to the front door of the home she was describing. As I drove there, I thought maybe I was being tricked...but it turned out to be true. There was a brand new house. It had four bedrooms, and was standing in an area that had been totally cleared of all trees. It seemed too good to be

205

true, given what I had gone through. I called the realtor. She put me in touch with the owner. We talked. She gave me the code for the garage door. I pulled my van into the garage and told God thank you. Thank you for helping me know I was supposed to be where I was.

I unloaded the van again. This time there wasn't anyone scary watching me. I drove home, for the Thanksgiving Holiday, confident that my prayers had been answered, and that Hannah and I were going to be OK.

Unfortunately, our time in West Virginia was to be short lived.

After Christmas break, I took Hannah with me, actually against her wishes, and to be honest, against her father's wishes, to West Virginia. It was the week after Christmas, in the middle of her first year of high school.

Hannah and I spent one of her first few nights in her new state at a New Year's Eve party that was hosted by a friend I had made there. Tina had a son, who was Hannah's age. She had invited the entire freshmen class to her home to celebrate the New Year. Hannah made friends. I received a call from Hannah the next Monday, after her first day at school....she was upset. I was beside myself listening to her telling me about her first day at school. She told me she was worried she had upset new friends, because several people asked her to sit with her at lunch and she had to pick.

I began to realize she was describing a good problem. She had gone from total isolation in Kentucky to this awesome dilemma.

By the end of our conversation, I was ecstatic. I was also very worried. My worst fear was that we would move, and that I would be OK, and Hannah would struggle. What was happening was Hannah was doing great, and I was watching my boss implode. I told myself that I would be fine. That whatever happened, I could survive it, and we would make it through until Hannah had a chance to finish high school.

I was wrong.

The picture perfect situation I was given during the interviewing process was not exactly correct. The president was deeply embroiled in conflict with his board, particularly the chair. He had a difficult way about him, and often simply refused to do what was required to perform the role. He refused to wear tuxedos to formal events. He skipped events altogether if he did not like people who would be in attendance, leaving the chair of the president empty.

I reached out to my support system, those people I turned to for help and guidance. I knew I was not in the gracious administration I had just left at NKU. I believed it would still work out for me, and Hannah, and that I would be able to learn something along the way.

The weeks rolled on, and I watched the administration fracture into camps. I was invited to behave very badly and join one of the camps that was undermining the president. I did not take that bait. My role was to support the president, and I consistently told everyone that I would do that to the best of my ability. Behind closed doors, I counseled the president about the eventuality of his behavior if not altered. In one of the last discussions I had with him, I said, "This war with your board is going to cost you your presidency." He was not listening to me, or anyone else.

I went to Washington, DC to perform lobbying on behalf of the university in March. My plane had just landed and I was standing at the baggage claim waiting for my suitcase when my cell phone rang. It was late in the morning, and I was concerned because I knew Hannah was not supposed to have her phone on during the school day. When I answered, she was crying so hard, I could not understand her. My heart skipped a beat. I asked her to slow down. I asked if Megan, the Student Government president for the university who stayed at our home with her when I travelled, was OK. I began to understand some of the words she was able to choke out.

"Mom! Do you remember when you said that if Dr. Votruba retired, you would have to find another job?"

"Yes, Hannah. I do. I'm not following you."

"Mom!!!!!!! Will you have to find another job now?"

"Hannah, I do not know what you mean. What does this have to do with Dr. Votruba?"

"Well, mom, everyone is talking about how the president of your new school just quit! He isn't the president anymore. I hope that doesn't mean that you have to find another job. I love my new school. I do not want to move again!"

More sobbing ensued. My mind worked to process what I was learning. The man who had recruited me to join him, as a single mother, had resigned, without even talking to me.

Hannah asked me again what it all meant. Would we have to move again? I pulled myself together, took a deep breath, and lied to my beloved daughter.

"Hannah, everything will be fine. I will figure out what to do."

We hung up. I saw my red suitcase circling the carousel, now the only one left. I pulled it off, and headed into the restroom. I sat down on the floor of the stall, and vomited.

In the small town we were in, there was nowhere else for me to work. No place that I could imagine that would meet our financial requirements. I knew already that the group that had been undermining the president would never lobby to keep my contract active. We had just totally unpacked our house. I had actually paid someone to burn the packing boxes in the vacant lot across the street after the garbage service refused to take them. I had felt settled for what seemed like a few minutes. And now, I knew it was all for naught.

After getting sick, I realized there was no reason now for me to go to Capitol Hill. I had no message to communicate since the president was no longer in office. I would learn later that he had headed to the place where the board chair had a business in town, and thrown down a letter of resignation after a disagreement. He showed them. They did not bargain with him to stay. He was welcomed to leave.

I made one phone call. It was to a man who was serving as a president in the DC area, and was someone I turned to often for advice. When he came to the phone, I said, "He just quit!"

We had spoken often about the tenuous place I had landed in, and the landscape that I was now part of. He said, "That isn't a funny joke." I told him I was not joking. This was real. He grew very somber. He then said he would clear his calendar to meet with me.

I was far more upset than my friend was. He was actually very calm. He said that if I played in the big leagues long enough, this sort of thing would eventually happen.

When I returned to West Virginia, exactly what I had expected happened. I first was told that I would be reassigned to a vice president. She had been undermining the president from the time that I arrived on the scene. The provost, who met with me, had originally told me that she was being asked to ascend to the role of interim president. Her first order of business would be to clean house, and take the vice president in question out of her role. I was disappointed to learn that in the eleventh hour she made a deal with the devil, and did not do that.

I stood my ground. I knew that my contract was to be a direct report to the president.

After a few agonizing days, I was told that I would remain a direct report to the president, but there really was no need for me to return to campus. My contract would not be renewed. It was March, so that left me and Hannah exactly ninety days of oxygen until I could get us to a new place. I was terrified.

I call the next few weeks of my life the, "Sleepless in Seattle and Doritos" period when I speak about it in public.

I would wake up each day, and take Hannah to school. I would then drive home to pop in, "Sleepless in Seattle" and lay on the couch, crying so the tears ran into my ears, and eat one bag of Doritos after another.

It is no surprise that this approach did not exactly help anything.

My daughter, Hannah, who did not even want to move in the first place, rescued me. One day after I picked her up from school, she scowled at me, and said, "Mom, you are freaking me out. You look a wreck. You need to take a shower. I have no idea what to do if you have no idea what to do."

So I confessed. I told her that the only way we would be able to financially survive was to pack the house and move wherever I could find work again. That I had seen an opportunity in Orlando, Florida, but that was so much farther away. And I was not sure, at all, that I could sell myself after such a short tenure in West Virginia.

She responded in a way I will never forget. She was excited. She said, "I love the ocean! Orlando will be great! We moved once. We can do it again. I will help. Let's go!"

It was not lost on me that she had moved forward light years from just six months before.

I went upstairs and got in the shower for the first time in a few days. I was feeling better. When I emerged, I thought I heard water continue to run. Puzzled, I walked out into the hallway in my towel. I walked down the stairs, and into the great room, where the kitchen and living room adjoined. Horrified, I saw what looked like a waterfall coming through the ceiling, pouring water onto the kitchen island, finding its' way into a small river, and then snaking down the stairs to the garage.

A pipe had come apart. Of course it was not the pipe that carried clean water. It was the pipe beneath my shower that carried the water going down the drain. I did the mental math in my head and thought about how many pots, pans, and dishes were inside the large kitchen island.

I literally lost my mind. I mean, like, in the scene from, "Baby Boom" where Diane Keaton learns that once again it will ONLY be SIX THOUSAND DOLLARS to fix a problem at her new, country home. I found myself walking around in the front yard, barefoot and clad only in a towel, screaming at the sky. Really?!!! I kept asking. Really. Yup. Really!

I sent an email to the person listed in Orlando for the new role as a National Dean for Medical Imaging Programs. I received an almost immediate response. I had also tentatively reached out to a University in Florida about a Chief of Staff position there. They also had immediately responded. My spirits lifted.

As it turned out, I was invited to visit with the opportunity in Orlando in short order. I flew down and looked at the locations for both opportunities. I saw a community that I thought was a better fit for Hannah in an Orlando suburb. The decision was made for me when I called the principal of the school that I had identified would be the best fit for her. I called on the Friday before Memorial Day and was shocked to get the principal on the phone. I explained my situation. I told him that Hannah definitely needed to be a part of the Color Guard, which supports the band. I understood that tryouts were over, that she had just tried out, and won a spot in West Virginia, but we were going to have to move in order to accept a new job opportunity. He told me he would look into it, and promised a call back soon. I was stunned when my phone rang about an hour later.

It was the band director. He displayed incredible empathy. Said he was aware of how disruptive an employment gap could be with regard to family, and shared that he had been in a similar situation. He told me that Hannah had a spot on the team. Period.

I called the Florida University and withdrew from the search process. I accepted the position in Orlando. And got into transition mode.

I went to Lake Mary, Florida, and found a house I loved. It would take a herculean effort to finance it after the financial fallout of the divorce. I got a contract in place, and went back to West Virginia in much better spirits.

As the financing process played out, I was notified that there was a stumbling block that might impede the closing. I was undeterred. I continued to forge ahead.

My real estate agent told me that the seller's agent, Miguel, was unable to speak English well, and it was difficult for her to communicate with him. That he sent voicemails that were hard to understand, and that she was worried he did not understand the delays that were recurring as I frantically worked to get everything cleared to close. If we passed the deadline that was identified on the contract, it would be dead, and I would have to resubmit another bid.

Upon returning to Florida, I drove by the house I knew was supposed to be mine. There was a sign in the yard that announced a yard sale the coming Saturday. I contacted my real estate agent and she told me that I absolutely should not show up at that event.

I did.

I wandered into the house I loved, filled with people, and looked around. A kind woman approached me. The yard sale was in full swing. She identified herself as the property manager. Her name was Saida, and she took care of everything for the owner during the leasing of the home. Now she was seeing things through to completion for the closing.

I told her I was the buyer pursuing the house, but my agent and I were having trouble communicating with the real estate agent from their side. She asked, "Do you mean, Miguel?"

"Yes! Do you know him?"

I was shocked when she pointed across the room to a man sitting at the kitchen table. She then said, "He is my son. He is sitting right there."

I walked over and said hello. In perfect English, Miguel said, hello to me. I then said, "My name is Kimberly Luse. I am the buyer for this property. Is there a reason why you have been calling my agent and acting like you cannot understand her and insisting on speaking only in Spanish?"

He looked mortified. It worsened when his mother began to chastise him. She then turned to me and said she had heard the financing had fallen through on my end, and that he was waiting out the contract because a friend of his had offered cash for the house.

I told her the truth. That I was a single mother, and needed the house because it was in the school district that my daughter needed. That I was alone in Florida, actually did not know a single person other than the people who hired me at my job, and now I was in jeopardy of losing the house. My furniture was on the truck, and on the way. I was nearly desperate because I had no idea where I would store the furniture because they were insistent that the truck would be unloaded or I would be charged an exorbitant amount of extra money.

Saida asked for my phone number. Later that day she did an extraordinary thing. To this day, I will always be grateful for her act of kindness. My phone rang, and she asked me if it would help to unload all of my furniture into the house's three-car garage. A full three days before the closing.

I began to cry, and told her that yes, that would save me and Hannah. My realtor was incredulous. So was the banker. Both of them spoke to me about the fact that foreclosures were at an all-time high in the state of Florida. So many people were having trouble with people renting homes, and then refusing to pay for them. That it took months to evict someone in that scenario. They marveled that the owner, and her property manager would take such a risk on me. He said that once I had the keys to the house, I could walk in and sit down my purse and under the state laws of Florida they would have to evict me if I decided not to move forward with the house closing.

I met Saida later that same day, and she handed me the keys to the front door. I drove over to the house, put the key in the door, walked into the home, and closed the front door behind me. I sat my purse down on the floor, and began to weep in gratitude. The closing was cleared for two days later, and I finally felt that I had secured a safe space for Hannah and me. It was such a long journey to that moment.

Evan drove Hannah down a few weeks later, as it got closer to band camp and the start of school. I remember well how excited Hannah was with the house, and her bedroom. Evan was very complimentary. My birthday falls on July the 4th. Evan, Hannah and I went to Daytona Beach on that day, and watched as fireworks were set off the pier. Hannah had started talking with a group of teenagers and had gotten herself invited to play volleyball. I was grateful beyond words that things had settled down. The only twinge I felt that was not positive was when it was time for Evan to leave. It would become a pattern that would last for years. Me, standing and watching as Evan departed, and knowing that it was not right. We were not supposed to be apart. And yet, here we were.

At the end of her freshmen year, Hannah performed with the school choir in West Virginia at the final choral concert in May. I sat in the audience very emotional, because she had just gotten settled and I was about to move her again. Three high schools in 18 months. One year later, I was sitting in the auditorium in her new high school in Lake Mary, Florida, again watching her perform in the final choral concert of the school year. The finale was the combined choirs singing, "When You Wish Upon A Star" acapella. It was beautiful, and the simple message was so meaningful. I was alone in the audience, which always made me a little sad. I wished that Hannah's Dad and other family members could be with us.

The time went by quickly. Hannah flourished in her new school. She fell in love with her American Sign Language classes, and as it turned out, exposure to that subject changed the course of her life. It would become the profession she would pursue as an adult.

During our second year in Florida, one of Hannah's dear friends, Monica, found herself in a very difficult home situation. Monica was a year older than Hannah, and a year ahead in school. We made the decision to take Monica into our home, where she also flourished. I was unprepared for the next chapter in our lives.

During an annual conference in Washington, DC, a trusted friend and colleague asked me how my new role was going. I told him I was fine, but it was not the large campus experience I was used to and frankly loved. My pay was also flat, with no increases. My expenses continued to climb, especially now that I was providing for two teenagers. He had an intriguing proposition.

He shared that a good friend of his was being named a new Chancellor. She had asked him to join her as her Chief of Staff. He was reticent to make a lateral move, as he was already serving in that role at another university in the state. He recommended that she talk with me. Things began to happen very quickly.

When I met his friend, things seemed too good to be true. I was offered the role and went home to discuss things with Hannah and Monica. Monica had just recently graduated high school and was beginning college that fall. Hannah would be starting her senior year. We discussed the practicality of me moving to the new location by myself, and having them stay behind. I shared with them the financial benefit for all of us, and if we could make that situation work for nine short months, they could then move with me and go to college at my new school.

We decided it was a good decision to accept the offer. I was nervous, and very anxious to leave the girls, although I knew they would be alright. The day I drove away from our home to begin the new adventure it was raining terribly. I backed the car out of the garage, and clearly remember Hannah standing in the doorway of the house, waving, and crying, as the garage door descended. I drove to the edge of the subdivision, and turned around. I went back to my house, and pulled in the driveway, and sat there for several minutes. I knew if I opened the garage door and went back in I would never, ever be able to leave. I told myself to be brave. I told myself to make one more big sacrifice in order to get all of us to a better place. I drove away, just a few days before my 50th birthday.

I rented a two bedroom apartment 638 miles north of my home in Florida. The far-too-familiar air mattress was back on the floor of my new place. I spent that milestone birthday alone, waking up on that mattress which at that point had developed a slow leak. It was very lonely. I thought about my family, all of my children, my grandchildren, and Evan. I wondered again how I had gotten to the place where I was all alone again, and what, if anything, I could do to change things.

I threw myself into my role. Hannah and I connected several times a day. When possible, I flew back to see her perform at the football games. Several weekends she came to see me. One trip, Monica came as well and they went to campus and hung out with the students there. Work was demanding, and the days went quickly. I began to think we were going to pull it off. And before long, I would be able to bring the girls with me for good, and we would be that much closer to home, which would make it easier to get back to Northern Kentucky for family events, and to visit more often.

I began to secretly worry as I saw the familiar signs of a dysfunctional administration at work. I told myself that God surely would not have led me to this opportunity if it was also going to fall through.

Fall through it did. In a way that was so spectacular, it nearly defined my life. I stood my ground on ethical issues that would violate my moral compass to its' core if I gave in. I quickly found myself on the outside of the circle. Shortly after the New Year, I was informed that I no longer was needed in my role. It was late in the evening, on a cold winter's night. It made no sense whatsoever. I spent an hour with my boss, getting direction as to what to do with the stack I had that was asking for response or representation. I went to my car, got in it, and headed south. I only stopped for gas, driving through the dark night until I pulled back into the garage of my home in Florida. I shared with the girls what had happened, and fell into bed, exhausted.

The next several months were ones of total panic for me. I tried to the best of my ability to shield the girls from the reality that I was running out of funds. My paycheck was stopped, and it was at the worst possible time in the academic year to secure a new position. I also now had two short tenures at universities which were overshadowing my true work ethic, and abilities, to potential employers.

I filled out 89 applications. I prayed. I cried. I begged and pleaded with God to help me. As spring began, I knew that I would have to sell the home I loved and had felt secure in. I was beyond any capacity to pay for it going forward, and no real prospects that were fleshing out to make me think things would improve financially.

I listed the house for sale. A contract came in during the first weekend. I signed it, and told the girls we had to move.

Hannah's graduation day approached. Our family came to Florida to celebrate the big event. I had promised her we would have the graduation party in our house, so I made a deal with the buyers to allow us to stay past that weekend. We had a big bash, and then it was all over. I stood and watched as Jessica and Kevin, and the grandchildren left. Sara, now pregnant with her first child, left as well. I felt like the world was closing in. My mother stayed behind a few more days, which was good for me. After the party, I looked at her, and said, "I don't know where to begin. I have to be packed, and out in four days."

She calmly said, "You just have to start somewhere." She then took a picture off the wall. We began to work on taking the house apart. I had contracted for two PODS to come. It was all I could afford. In the end, whatever I could not fit in the PODS was given away to Habitat For Humanity, Goodwill, and even to some of Hannah's friends. Monica took a bed. She was returning home to her father's house. Jeanine was another young lady who had stayed with us from time to time. She was putting together an apartment, and we dropped off furniture for her to use. It felt good knowing the things were going to good use. I had no idea how I would replace everything. It was the best solution I could manage at the time.

We sold the house, and netted some money. I had been progressing in a search process in Georgia, and walked away from our Lake Mary home grateful for the time we had there. I worried I might never be able to provide another safe place again for myself and my family.

Oftentimes throughout that period, I woke up in a terrified state. I had a recurring nightmare. In it, Hannah and I were running through a misty night, and there was a monster close at our heels. I tried house after house, never finding anywhere that was safe to get us away from the danger. It would be several years before it subsided.

I let myself think about an idea I had. I wondered if I might be able to start my own company, and be the master of my own destiny. I had a friend, who after being down-sized had done that very thing. I let fear hold me back, and kept applying to positions as I traditionally had.

I also was grappling with the fact that my youngest was now a high school graduate, and I was going to be an empty nester. Hannah went home to Kentucky for the summer. I did as well, and was sitting in my Mother's house when I received a phone call. It was right before my birthday, on July 2nd. I was offered another Chief of Staff role for a university in Georgia. I thought how much had transpired in the twelve short months since the offer for that role had been extended the summer before. I accepted the offer, and used the rest of my funds to buy a home near my new school. I started back over with the relocation process. New license. New cable. New utilities. Unpacking and getting settled once again. Telling myself it was all for the best. I was geographically close to Hannah, as she was a few hours drive south in college, and I was closer to my family in Kentucky.

As the academic year began, I found myself in such a lonely place. I was alone in a four-bedroom house. The extended visits that had occurred when the grandchildren were younger had stopped now that they were in preschool and had schedules of their own. Hannah would drive up from time to time, and stay for the weekend. When she left, I could hardly bear the silence.

I also did not fit in well in the environment I found myself in. I was in a very small town, with very traditional viewpoints and values. Political incorrectness was rampant. I told my mother once that I would as likely find a unicorn walking down the sidewalk as another woman my age who was single by choice. I was invited to church, and to be set up on blind dates on a nearly daily basis.

As I attended my first large event, I was mortified when a colleague introduced me to the group as a northern sympathizer. He went on to say, "But, hey guys, she's easy on the eyes, so we can forgive her I guess!"

I struggled to keep any muscle in my face from moving. There is no correct response to a remark like that.
I went to the local car dealership to purchase a vehicle. The salesman immediately asked me if my husband was coming to help me. I replied that was unlikely. I pointed to the car I wanted to test drive. His response? "Well, ma'am, I am not comfortable with that. You see, that car is a stick-shift."

So I asked him what were we talking about? What type of gear knob was it? On the column? On the floor? Did it have an overdrive?

He took a full two steps backwards and looked at me as if I had just had my head turn backwards. It took a little while, but I did eventually test drive a few cars. The terrible, unsettled feeling intensified.

I tried to silence the voice in my head that began to whisper that I still was not in the right place. I unpacked my boxes, and hung everything up for the fourth time since leaving the home I shared with Evan.

Compounding issues for me was the fact that I had done most of the lifting and packing for the previous two moves on my own. I had damaged my cervical spine in the process. A visit to the doctor brought sobering news. I needed immediate surgery to stabilize two slipped discs and a vertebra that was displaced.

I decided to wait until Thanksgiving break so as not to disrupt my new role as soon as I arrived. It was a frightening time. The surgery occurred and I found myself in a very large cervical collar, trying to handle everything.

The familiar politics were at play in this new situation. By that point, I was able to isolate behaviors and predict who might be successful and where the road was going to end for others. I began to realize that the president was not going to survive unless he took specific action against some of his executive team. As time wore on, I knew he was not going to do that.

A fateful night occurred the Friday before spring break week that did not only change the course of my life. It nearly ended it.

I was not feeling well that week. A visit to the doctor left me feeling discouraged. My neck, which originally had gotten much better after the surgery, had begun to hurt again. He recommended that I start taking Lyrica, to handle the constant, nagging pain. I did not really pay attention to the warnings that outline feelings of depression or suicide might ensue. I had symptom relief which was encouraging, but felt myself going down a dark hole at the same time. Looking back, I now know that I was impaired by the medication in a way that prevented me from understanding exactly what was happening to me. All I knew for sure was that I was just not myself.

There was a black-tie event on campus that particular Friday, hosted by the president. It was a fundraiser and I knew I had to attend. That morning, I did text the president and asked to be excused from a meeting on campus. I shared that I was not feeling well. I had just flown back from Washington, DC, was planning to go to Orlando for the weekend, and was due back to Washington, DC on Monday. I wanted to be sure I could make it through the evening's activities.

I rested in the morning and then went to have my hair professionally fixed for the party. My hairdresser said she could see I was not doing well. I talked with her about being placed on Lyrica. I went home, and got ready to go. I had a formal black dress that was tea-length, beautiful shoes, and I put my best face on. I was acutely aware that I was all alone again. I thought again about how I used to go to all those types of events with Evan, when my life made sense, and I was working at NKU.

I went to the ball. I had talked with the Provost earlier in the week about how isolated I felt there. He suggested that I try to go out after work with some of my coworkers to try to get to know people better. I was an outsider. Most people there were from that area and had deep connections to one another through work, church, and their children's activities. For months, I had not been able to break into the inner circle.

I had dinner, and some wine. I danced and put on a brave face and hoped no one could tell just how badly I felt physically, and how much of an outsider I considered myself.

Towards the end of the evening, something happened that had never happened there before. I was invited to the after party! I thought about the fact that I had promised Hannah that I would drive down to Orlando in the very early morning to spend the weekend and watch her color guard competition. I knew it would make for a late night, and I would be tired. The Provost's words played through my memory. I told them I would love to go out afterwards. The catch was the ballroom needed to be torn down by one of the members of the group, so there was a bit of a wait before they were heading out.

I took off my heels, and tried to rest my neck and back. I sat down at a table, and put my feet up and began to work on emails. Finally, it was time to go.

It was a beautiful evening, and by this point it was quite late. We were on a large campus, and I was frequently lost, day and night. Directionality has never been my strong suit. It was somewhat of a running joke. I walked with the group to a parking lot that I had not seen before. It was out of the back side of the Student Center, and wound through the campus. I did not pay a lot of attention to the dark buildings we were passing along the way. I was tired, and thinking that the wine seemed to have hit me hard for some reason. I never put together the equation that Lyrica played into that evening. I thought about Hannah again, and changed my mind at the last minute about going out.

I told the small group I was walking with that I was sorry, but that I really had better get myself home, and ready to leave in the morning. I had to be on the road by 7am if I was going to make it to the first round of competition in Orlando.

They all said they understood. The head of program events then offered me a bottle of liquor that was in bags some of them were carrying. I was surprised, because it was opened, and had been served at the dance. I questioned her, and she told me that she always took the unused liquor after events because it would just be wasted if she did not take it.

I actually do not normally buy hard liquor. I thought it was a nice gesture, though, so I took it. I turned around and began to walk back in the direction of the Student Union. I was parked in front of it. I had made the decision that I would get my computer out of my car, and call a cab just to be sure I would not be driving impaired. My thoughts slowed down a little when I realized how deadly silent and quiet, the campus was. It was after 11pm and I suddenly realized I was totally alone. I grew scared, and turned around and walked quickly back to where I had left the group. I got there just in time to see the taillights of the last car pulling away.

Part of my role had been to monitor the calls to the campus police department, and make judgements about when to notify the campus community in the event that something dangerous had happened. I began to think about the recent robberies, where victim's cell phones were taken from them, or worse. The fact that there was a lot of drug activity and even gang activity began to run through my thoughts. I walked faster. I also was trying desperately to ignore the lifelong problem that was making things worse. I needed to find a restroom, but my pass card to get into any of the buildings was locked inside my car.

I continued to walk, and went the direction I thought would lead me back. I found myself somewhere else entirely. Every time the Spanish moss in the trees was stirred by the wind, I was sure that someone was coming out of the woods to get me. My heart was racing. I decided that the best thing to do was totally back track, and start over again from the parking lot where my colleagues had been. Therefore, I walked back.

I turned around and made a conscious effort to go a different direction along the walkway hoping it would take me to my car. I also had a terrible reality occurring. I needed to use the bathroom. Badly. My building pass was in my car, and I could not find my car. I was desperate. As I was walking the familiar tipping point came, and I felt urine begin to spill. I had protection on, but before long, it was not enough to hold the amount I was losing. As I walked, the urine began to splash on the walkway. I was mortified, but also very aware that I had no ability to stop it. I did what I could to walk in a way to save my shoes. Mercifully, it finally stopped, and I was able to regain control.

It was then that I heard voices. I turned around and I saw the campus police. I was never so happy to see anyone in my life. I thought they would help me. They were not there to help.

They questioned what I was doing. I told them I was lost, and needed help getting back to my car. One of the officers asked, "Are you carrying an open bottle of liquor?"

I replied, that yes, I was given it after the dance by the head of event services. That I was not drinking it, it had been handed to me already opened.

I remember being so grateful that my accident had happened before they had arrived, as it would have been so very embarrassing explaining my medical issues.

They showed me the way to my car, and I opened the hatch, and put the bottle inside. I took off my shoes, and looked up what cab services were available there. I was shocked to learn there was one single cab driver worker that night. For the whole city. I gave them my location and began to wait.

More than once, the officers said I looked so tired. They encouraged me to just open my car door and have a seat inside until the cab came. I was suspicious, because they were not being friendly, or supportive. I also have a good friend who had shared a terrible story with me. She was travelling, and was in a hotel, and walked outside from the restaurant to sit in her car, and charge her phone for a few minutes. She was parked in the lot, not moving, in a hotel whose staff knew her well. Security for the hotel knocked on her window, and arrested her for driving under the influence, even though she was not driving anywhere. It resulted in her being handcuffed, and taken to the police station.

I wondered what the officers were trying to do to me in that scenario. I was not at all convinced they were worried about me being tired, needing to sit down.

Time drug on, and I decided to text the Provost's wife. Their house was very close to mine, and I considered the Provost a friend. I asked if they were still up. She said they were and put her husband on the phone. I explained what had happened and asked if he would simply come and pick me up. I could come back in the early morning for my car.

Not long afterwards, both the Provost and his wife showed up. I rode with her, and he drove my car to my house. Problem solved, or so I thought.

I was up very early, and headed to Orlando. I had a great Saturday with Hannah, and we stayed at a nice hotel together and caught up. On Sunday, things began to change.

A trusted friend who was a reporter for the local newspaper called me. He told me I needed to be careful. He shared that people that should have no access to the police reports for the university were calling him asking him to hold the front page of the paper for a story. A terrible story about me. He said they were rewriting parts of the report from the Friday before. He said, quite ominously, "There appears to be blood in the water, and it is yours. I don't know what is going on, but it isn't good."

A short while later my cell phone rang. It was the president. I was originally relieved. He had a strict rule that I was not to bother him after hours. I thought I would now have the opportunity to share with him what had transpired and get a jump on talking to him about the strange series of events before Monday morning.

I was stunned by his message. He was very formal, and told me he was aware of the incident the evening of the gala, and I was on administrative leave until further notice. I tried to speak, but he refused to let me say anything. He then hung up.

Hannah kept asking for the remainder of the afternoon if I was OK. I kept saying I was. I was far from OK. I knew that if the president had already been behind closed doors with others, and did not even allow me to speak, that it was already too late.

I marveled at the man I had worked so hard for. I marveled that he had not once asked if I was OK. I marveled that he would have no empathy at all, or wonder what must have happened to me that Friday. I began to spiral down to a place that was terrifying at the end.

I told Hannah goodbye and drove back to my house. I sent a message to the meeting organizers that I would not be in DC the following morning. I waited. And waited. And waited.

Shortly before 5pm, an email arrived in my inbox, summoning me to the president's office. I drove the familiar route, parked in my usual spot, and walked in. The vice president over the Human Resources department was waiting with him. I took a deep breath, and walked in.

I watched the two of them do everything you should never, ever do from an HR perspective. The president asked me if I would like to resign. He would not listen to anything I had to say. His vice president told me it was a, "dark day" for the university. Neither of them seemed to have any empathy for me, or what I had just experienced. It took a little while before I discovered they did not even have the correct information. But absent allowing me to talk, they would have to receive it in a much more difficult, and career ending fashion.

I picked up the pen and the president told me, word for word, what to write. In shock, I wrote the sentences and got up. I walked into my office, where I was able to gather my belongings in just a few moments. I had learned long ago to not trust any employer too much, and to always be ready to pack if that scenario arose.

I drove the short distance back to my house. All the prior experiences ran through my mind. I walked around and around my lonely home. I had no idea how I would ever pack and start back over again. I felt lost in a way that I never have before.

I took my Lyrica. I then looked at that big bottle of pills. I went to the restroom, and pulled out the narcotic painkillers and realized I had a lot of them as well. A dark plan began to formulate inside my mind.

I did not call anyone at home to share what had just happened. I went to bed, and stayed there until the next day. I drew the curtains, and was overwhelmed at the cruelty of people. Stories had started to circulate on social media. I was taunted on platforms such as Twitter.

The Provost and one other colleague reached out. No one else showed any sort of support. The stories were incredible. One version had me stripped naked, and in the fountain on the great lawn when the police showed up. I later learned that in my terrified walk back and forth that the police officers had actually followed me prior to making their presence known. The police report had been pulled the day after and rewritten to include salacious remarks about me, "toting a bottle of liquor, and urinating on the sidewalk." There were stories that described people looking for my shoes and clothes in the woods. It was beyond ridiculous, but it was out there just the same.

By Thursday, I had decided I just would not continue. With anything. I could not imagine dealing with the shame I was feeling, and the rejection that was so blatant. I poured out the contents of my bottles of pills, and began taking them a few at a time.

As this process went on I was gathering pictures of my family and putting them in a nest of sorts in my bed. I wrote letters apologizing to my family. I wrote a long one to my mother. I apologized, and said I had tried. I was just simply too tired to go on.

My friend, Laura, began to text me during that terrible day. At first, I was texting back. As the afternoon wore on, I went into my bedroom, climbed under the covers, laid my head down for what I expected was the last time. I looked at the pictures surrounding me. I prayed for forgiveness. A welcome fog began to set in.

From somewhere that seemed very far away, I heard yelling, and pounding. It continued. I struggled to sit up, and then put my feet on the floor. Everything tipped. The space between the bed and the doorway was exaggerated, and seemed very long. The walk across the great room was difficult, and distorted.

I opened the door, and there stood Laura, a look of absolute panic on her face. Behind her, a life squad was pulling up to the curb. I looked at her, and pleaded. Told her I would be OK. I would not take anything else, just please send them away.

She looked doubtful. I had to vomit, which helped to clear some of the pills I had taken out of my system. She sent the squad away, and explained to them that she had overreacted. She came in and sat with me for a long, long time.

I cried. I told her I did not know how to move forward. There was no place to retreat to. I was lost and alone.

About that time, I received a message from the Provost's wife. She had returned to their home in Tampa, and she insisted I come down there and stay for a while. She wanted me to have relief from the cruelty of the community I was trapped in.

I assured Laura I would do just that. I also threw away all the remaining pills.

It would be a few days before I would see a commercial warning against the side effects of Lyrica. Suicidal thoughts or actions might occur. Alcohol may intensify side effects.

I will never know how much it contributed to my actions that terrible day, but I remain convinced it was a huge factor.

I went to Tampa. I slept, and swam, and sat on the beach. I thought about the previous few years, and tried to sort it out. Three boats were on the horizon in front of me one sunny afternoon. Three boats! I looked up at the sky, and prayed to ask if this was the answer.

I remembered the joke about a priest, and a minister, and a rabbi who were travelling on a ship that sank. One by one, three boats came by, each offering to help. Each time, they responded, "No thank you, God is going to save us!"

They eventually drowned, and when they reached heaven's gates they asked why God had not saved them after all.

The response? "I sent you THREE boats!"

I had wondered for several years about starting my own business. For three years to be exact. For several years, I had gone home to visit, and then cried all the way to the airport when it was time to leave. I knew I was in the wrong place. I knew I was working in environments that were out of alignment with my personal moral compass. I had let fear hold me back from trying.

I thought of my good friend, whose business was thriving. I called her and asked if she thought I was smart enough to do it, too. Teri laughed at me. She said she knew I was, and that she was going to send me templates and materials to help me get the ball rolling. She gave me advice, and told me it appeared to be the time.

My thoughts had begun to clear. I found myself reaching out for help again. Making a plan.

I called Delta airlines from the beach. I asked if I could convert the ticket I had in reserve with them to fly home early for Easter. They told me I could. I booked it to depart from Tampa the following day.

I then called my mother and told her I was coming home, and about to do something irresponsible. I was going to move back without a job. I was going to create one and make myself the Principal and Founder.

My phone rang later that afternoon. It was my friend and colleague, reporter from the local newspaper. He told me that in his due diligence to get to the bottom of the lurid details that were circulating he had performed an open records request, and asked to view the security camera's footage of the evening of the gala. I asked what he had discovered. I will always remember his answer:

"It is grainy and dark, but I could see that you walked out with a group of people, turned around and walked back alone, turned the wrong way, hesitated and then walked back to the parking lot, turned around and headed back again, and then the campus police showed up. Other than that, it showed that you were standing by your car, holding your shoes, and you were picked up. At no time did you look like you had lost your faculties. You looked lost."

He then shared with me that an investigation was in process to discover how people had obtained the report that had no right to have it, why it was rewritten, and how the employee who gave me the bottle of alcohol was still employed.

We talked about how best to move forward. He suggested I share my experience with the people at the system office in Atlanta. Before I did that, I called the head of the campus police, and asked what their investigation had revealed. I was told that they had concluded I had no way to know that it was not customary to take the left over alcohol home since it was my first event there, and that at no time did I appear to be unaware of what was happening. They had swept my texts and emails and been able to determine that I was working. She was kind to me. I requested a written copy of all of the materials and then decided I would reach out to the system office.

I was told that they had received notice that I had resigned for personal reasons and that they were surprised. They invited me to share what had happened to me.

I waited until the following morning, and submitted a long, honest account of what had transpired. I actually wrote it on my laptop from the kitchen table where I was staying with Elsa, the wife of the Provost. It was vulnerable, factual, and painful. I looked at the send button for a long time, but in the end, hit it, and then headed to the airport.

I went through security, got onto the plane, and felt more settled than I had in many, many weeks. I was going home, and this time I was going to stay there. I had no idea how I would do it, but I had a deep, abiding sense of peace that I was finally heading in the right direction.

The plane went up. The plane landed in northern Kentucky a few hours later. I powered my phone on and thought it was going to implode with all the incoming messages.

The first one I responded to was from my friend, the reporter for the paper. His message? "Did you have anything to do with this?"

I already knew that the system office was reinstating me and I was going to be paid through the balance of my contract.

What was new to me was a letter that had been released by the president to the university and community. He was announcing that he and his wife had decided it was time to step aside.

I realized, as I was reading it, that my decision to step forward helped bring the truth to light. I often speak to audiences about the price you pay if you come forward, and the price you pay if you do not. I know myself enough to understand that when I am on my deathbed if I have not spoken the truth, as I know it, I will be regretful. That price would be higher for me. Therefore, I pay the price of taking the heat and criticism when I do come forward. As time has gone along, I have found that others have benefitted from my sharing about these very difficult experiences. The most common reaction I have is one of wonderment. Most people who approach me say they thought they were alone in the world, and had no idea that anyone else was going through anything that was similar. The lesson I have learned is that we are not alone.

I went home, and went one by one to everybody in my family to share what had happened. Support poured out. I went to Evan's house, and shared with him as well. Told everyone how close I had danced to the edge, and that I never wanted to be there again. I needed help. I was learning to ask for what I needed.

I prepared for my sixth move to bring myself home. I returned to Georgia and retained a moving company, that would prove to be a disaster, to move me back home.

I had to literally go to my knees to understand what I was supposed to learn from the final move back. The movers I found were recommended to me, listed as a credible company on the state website. I lived in such a rural area; I could not find anyone willing to make the multiple hour drive to do a proper on sight walk through. I knew how it was supposed to work. I just could not manage to do it.

Long Haul Movers showed up the day of the move. At that point, I had leased the house to a couple relocating to work at Moody's Air Force Base, and their truck was on the way. I had to vacate. The movers walked in, and said they had not understood on the phone how big the job actually was. They doubled the price, immediately, and threatened to walk off the job if I did not agree. So I agreed.

I also expressed grave concern about the size of the moving truck in my driveway. I told them I had moved the contents four times before, and did not believe they could fit everything into that truck. They laughed at me, said they were experts, and could easily take care of things. Hour after hour we worked, shoulder to shoulder. Later that evening, I was told that the truck was not big enough.

Beyond the several thousand dollars increase from that morning, they wanted an additional $800 to bring a second truck the next morning. I refused. I told them I knew it was against federal law for them to increase the price once they had begun to load the truck. I was told I could take it up later with the owner.

In the morning they arrived, and said it would take just a few more hours to finish. The morning passed, and in the late afternoon, there was still a lot to do. I had to go to the post office, and forward my address as I was leaving that night.

I told them I would be right back and drove around the corner. I returned to find them gone. The house was a wreck, with garbage laying everywhere, and many things left that had not been loaded. I called the company. No one ever answered. I began to work to clean everything up so the people who had leased my house could arrive the next morning.

After several hours, I felt like the house was presentable. I then slowed down to look at the contract we had signed the day before. It was laying on the counter in my kitchen. They had altered it. Instead of the, $6,000.00 total that they had insisted on, they had taken a pen and drawn a zero above the first zero in the total, making it into an 8. So it added the additional $800 they had demanded late the evening before. They then scratched out all of the numbers in the totals below to reflect their new math. It was incredible.

I had no choice but to wait to find any sort of resolution. I focused on going home. I had taken a Loft in downtown Cincinnati, in a building that was the former Shillitos Department Store when I was young. I had such wonderful memories of visiting there at Christmas time with my family. It seemed like such a long way away to go to Cincinnati when I was a little girl! In reality, it was just across the bridge from our home. It was surreal...the sights and sounds of the big city. We went through the line, waiting to see Santa, through Santa Land, complete with animated reindeer and the workshop where the elves built the toys. It was magical.

All those years later, I returned, and walked into the management office, and asked about the possibility of leasing a unit. I told the manager my story. My connection with the building. My memories of my family. My father had long since died. I shared that I had no job, but that I was fun, would promise to pay my lease, and was building my own company. I was absolutely convinced that was where I was supposed to be.

The manager looked at me with a critical eye. Just like 1986, a total stranger took a chance on me. She told me to come back in a few hours and I could sign the papers. It was done.

Once I had the keys, I scheduled the delivery of my belongings. My situation with the terrible moving company grew more dire.

The day of the delivery, one small truck arrived, with two men who I had never met. They looked very scary. I had asked the lift elevator operator from the building to come to the loading dock to stand with me. We had met that very day, his name was Tyrone, and he would prove to be a guardian angel for me.

The driver of the truck demanded $800 additional dollars to open the door to the truck. Tyrone kept interjecting that he had never, in fifteen years, seen anything like what he was witnessing. I called the Cincinnati police. They advised me to pay it if I wanted to see my belongings again. They said I would need to take it up in court later.

I paid it. And when they were finished, it was clear all of my things were not on that truck. All of the boxes were crushed, and glass shards were falling out of every one of them. When I asked where the rest of my things were, I was assured another truck was coming.

It did not come that day. Or for the next ten days in a row. I went back to a hotel room, and counted my funds, hoping everything would hold together long enough for me to be successful in my transition home.

The weekend the first truck showed up was the Saturday before Labor Day. I walked down to my son in law's work the next day to see the big, annual fireworks display. I thought about that event 28 years before. When I went to my first, real date with Evan. I wondered if he was somewhere thinking about that night. Somewhere out there, beneath the pale moonlight.

When the rest of my things finally arrived, they were in the same condition as the contents of the first truck. Tyrone again was standing at my side, incredulous at what was taking place.

When it was all said and done, I had over $28,000.00 in theft, damages, and overcharges. I persisted, and won, a small claims lawsuit against Eli Shalem, and Long Haul Movers in Downey County, California. To date, they have never paid the fine. They simply went underground, and disbanded their company. They now are operating under another name, and claiming additional victims everyday.

As I unpacked box after box, I looked to the sky, and asked God, "Why?" Why was the ceramic plate my son made for me broken to bits? The vase that held the flowers at my father's funeral? What was I supposed to be learning?

I believe I was learning to let go. Everything material is actually not replaceable, but it is certainly not the most important thing. As painful as it all was, I learned to cherish the things that were left. The pictures that did arrive. The work that my mother and daughter put into gorilla gluing everything back together.

I put the loft together. It worked beautifully. Somehow, still, it was not home. I knew that as well as I knew my reflection in the mirror. I focused on recruiting clients, and building my business, but the nagging feeling that I was still not home continued.

I began to recruit clients. I landed a few, and began to build. I also began to listen to God and follow the pathway forward. That pathway was about to take me across the Atlantic Ocean.

Chapter 15 (2016) Lessons Learned from Falling out of the Bathtub on the Other Side of the World

You won't stop me
I am a fighter and I
I ain't goin' stop
There is no turning back
I've had enough~
Fighter, Christina Aguilera

I did fall out of the bathtub in Mauritania. It was a long way from Grand Avenue in Newport, where I grew up, to walking off the plane on the other side of the world. Again, I have my mother to thank for encouraging me to pursue the opportunity that had presented itself. By this point, I was purposefully following the signs of the universe, and trusting that I was going to be successful in building my company. Some signs, are simply more powerful than others, though.

And as much as I completely believe what I am writing, I must confess that an encounter I had in June, 2016, while riding in a cab in Washington, DC, is still somewhat rocking my world. I had a somewhat lengthy ride, and began chatting with the cab driver. He is from

Mauritania, Africa, and was very pleasant. He asked where I was from, and I told him I was living in Cincinnati. He replied that Cincinnati was one of his favorite areas in the United States. He then went on to say that he attended a college in that area and graduated in 2010. He said, "I found a school where the faculty cared about me and knew my name." Our eyes locked in the rear-view mirror, as I realized he was quoting from the often-used tagline that President Jim Votruba said about Northern Kentucky University. I asked, "Are you quoting Jim Votruba?" He replied, "Yes, do you know Jim Votruba? I walked across the stage and he handed me my diploma in May, 2010." I replied, "Not only do I know Jim Votruba, I was sitting on the stage behind him at commencement, in May 2010!"

I then asked Yacoub the question on my mind. "If you love Cincinnati, and have graduated from NKU, how has your journey led you to driving a cab in DC?"

He pulled the visor down and said to look at his license. That it was, in fact, only three days old. He was there helping his parents relocate to retire in DC, and was just picking up extra money before he returned to Mauritania. He had dual citizenship and spent time in the US, but works in the Mauritania, and has a big passion for elevating the healthcare system there. He said, "We are looking for help to open a new hospital in the capital city of Nouakchott. Do you know anyone who would be willing to travel there to assist us?"

I have actually never felt such a powerful feeling of being placed right in the pathway of a wonderful opportunity. I am a healthcare professional with thirty years of experience, and one thing my company does is assist hospital and healthcare facilities with issues such as quality assurance, compliance, and best practices in Human Resources. This cab ride ended with an exchange of contact information, and an invitation to me from the Minister of Heath's office to visit Mauritania and meet with the leaders in healthcare there three short weeks later. The visit was truly transformational.

I was happy that I had made the trip. I was moved by the human suffering I witnessed, and wanted to provide assistance to. I also had a truly terrifying episode that I will never forget.

I arrived, and was exhausted. I really had no idea what to expect. I walked off the plane, entered the airport, and was surrounded by men, armed with very big guns. They were speaking loudly, and I could not understand anything they said. My crash course in French was not serving me well. I was grateful when a man unfolded a wrinkled paper that had my name printed on it. I nodded. Yes, that was me.

We went through customs at the airport, sometimes, clearly cutting corners. I walked out to meet the Chief of Staff to the Minister of Health. He was standing there in a long, flowing, white robe. He spoke very little English. He motioned me to a jeep that was waiting. I climbed in, and we headed out across a rudimentary road into the desert. I was worried.

At nearly every mile marker, a man with a large gun waved our car aside, and then, apparently recognizing my driver, waved us through.

I began to relax, understanding that I was under the protection of the government. I was with Cheikh. He was gracious, and took me home to his family to have my first meal in that country. I was fond of his wife and daughter. His daughter and I discovered that we both had Katy Perry our playlist.

At the end of my first day there, I was able to take a shower. I was so happy that I had made the decision to go there, and the water that fell over me was so wonderful. I truly thought I had never felt anything as refreshing in my life. That is when the unexplainable happened. I leaned forward to pick up my shampoo bottle, and lost my balance. In a crazy, slow-motioned, fast-forwarded fashion I literally skied across the bathtub, arms wind milling, grasping for anything I could find. I made a three quarters turn, and fell backwards. I found myself laying on the bathroom floor, knees caught on the bathtub ledge, shower curtain and rod laying on top of me, as the water continued to pour on.

It was on omen of sorts.

As the days went along, I grew increasingly uncomfortable with Cheikh's insistence that we meet in closed rooms to discuss my progress. A frightening day came towards the end of my time there.

As we were talking about moving the project forward, Cheik moved over to sit very close to me. He then placed his arm around my neck. I stood up. I told him that I was there to work. Period.

He then proclaimed his love for me. He told me that he wanted me to consider that he would be my man in Mauritania. I was incredulous. I told him he did not even know me. He said that I had no man in America, so what was the problem? I thought about Evan, and knew I did have someone out there. I was also acutely aware that I was with a government official, in Mauritania, behind closed doors. It would be my word against his if it came to that.

He became belligerent. He stood up, yelling. He said, "You are a woman, and you will sit down and respect me!"

I thought back, in that moment to everyone who told me not to go to Mauritania. I wondered if that was going to be the end. I then heard my mother's voice. She was the last person I spoke to before I walked onto the plane to travel there. "Do not let anyone there intimidate you."

I took a deep breath. I said, "I am an American woman and you will respect me too."

I was terrified.

He looked confused. His eyes told the story that he was in unchartered waters. I remembered one lesson from my self-defense classes, and took a small step towards him. I looked straight into his eyes and said, "Do you understand me?"

A flicker appeared in his eyes. This was not how he expected things to go. I felt a tiny flame of encouragement. I straightened my back and held my ground.

He retreated. He asked me not to tell anyone what had taken place. I agreed. He left. I went to the floor, shaking. I truly felt that I had stared down the dragon, and that if my bluff had failed, I could have landed in real trouble.

I came back from that experience and relaunched the name of my company. Going forward we would be known as, Strategic Ethical Solutions, International. At times, I block out time to do nothing other than explore to see who I am supposed to connect with on any given day. Not long ago I was in Krogers, racing thought the aisles, and almost crashed my cart into the cart of a man who turned a corner in front of me.

I apologized. I raced back off, and a few minutes later, rounded another corner, and this time, did crash my cart into the same man. We both began to laugh. I said, "Well apparently we are supposed to meet. Let's try and figure out why!"

He replied, "So you graduated from Clemson University?" I was puzzled for a few seconds, and then realized I was wearing a Clemson sweatshirt. I explained I was a consultant, and Clemson was one of my clients. He then stepped back, and said that his wife worked in the local school system, and was in need of a consultant with expertise in the educational field. I looked up, and smiled. Another sign. Another boat, if you will.

Lessons learned. Each human interaction is ripe with bondless opportunities to connect and network to wonderful new adventures. In this age of racing around, and getting pulled into a cell phone screen while you are walking, or riding in a cab, or even sitting in a restaurant...resist falling into that behavior. It is a true oxymoron that the connectivity that technology offers also leads to true isolation and missed opportunities to connect with the person standing right in front of you. Be aware, and listen to the universe. It is amazing what happens when you do. It would not be long before listening to that higher power led me back to reconnect to the most meaningful relationship in my lifetime.

Chapter 16 (2017) Finally Home

The story of my life is very plain to read. It starts the day you came. And ends the day you leave. The story of my life begins and ends with you. The names are still the same, and the story's still the truth. I was alone. You found me waiting and made me your own. I was afraid that somehow I never could be, the one that you wanted of me. You're the story of my life. And every word is true. Each chapter sings your name, each page begins with you. It's the story of our times, and never letting go. And if I die today, I wanted you to know. Stay with me here. Share with me, care with me, stay and be near. And when it began, I'd lie awake every night. Just knowing somewhere deep inside, that our affair just might write. The story of my life. Is very plain to read. It starts the day you came. It ends the day you leave. ~The Story of My Life, Neil Diamond

2017 began quietly for me. I had committed to writing a book, but found I was hitting unexpected walls. It would take nearly the entire year to pass before I discovered why I did not realize my goal of completing it by July.

Right after the New Year, I received a message from Ej. I had not been in touch with him for more than a year. There were several devastating events during the holiday season of 2015, where near overdoses were being publicized on Facebook. It was tearing our entire family apart, and I finally sent a message to him, begging him to get help, and reminding him that he had full medical coverage, and a family who cared about him. I then drew a line in the sand, and said that I would be disengaging until something positive happened.

Something positive did happen. I received a message from Ej, and he communicated something that he had not said for the previous dozen years. His message? "I have a problem. I do not want to live this way anymore. I need help."

I knew I could not help him on my own. I called his father. I asked for help. We went together the next day and picked him up. For the balance of the day, things went well. Ej was sincere, and he agreed to go to the hospital as a first matter of course. He was in a very fragile physical state.

Hours passed as the hospital workers assessed his physical condition. It was so difficult for me, as his mother, to see what a tenuous situation he was in physically. I prayed, and did what I do best. I began to network, and bargain with people at the best inpatient facility in the region that treats mental health and addiction issues. I landed a bed, at a very late afternoon hour, at that very facility. Ej was ready to go, and I was so relieved. I even allowed myself to think about the future, and see him back with our family. Back in his rightful place. In so many ways, his journey mirrored the prodigal son in the bible. The son who had lost his way, but whose family always prayed for his return. I hoped this was the break in the dam that would allow that to happen.

Ej drifted off into a fitful sleep. He awoke, and I was sitting there by his bed in the Emergency Room. Evan had stepped out. It was a triage set up so there were many cubicles with beds surrounding a general nursing station.

My stomach clenched when I saw the look on his face as he fully awakened. He was going into a familiar rage that I had experienced many times before. I stood up. He sat up, and began cursing and yelling at me. Everyone came running back to our space. Evan looked devastated when he saw what was happening.

Ej was screaming that I had tricked him. That he knew all along that I would do anything to trick him, and commit him. He knew he could never, ever trust me. He began to walk towards the doorway to the exit. It was less than 10 degrees outside that night, it was late, and he did not even have a decent coat on. I managed to say, "Ej, you are making a mistake."

He turned at the door, and yelled back to me, "If you want to see the biggest mistake that was ever handed to me in my life, take a long look in the mirror."

He walked out into the darkness. I sat down, trembling, and began to cry. Evan tried to console me. I took out all of my frustration from the last many, many years on Evan that night. Told him that maybe if he had held a stronger line with Ej we would not have been in this situation. Evan looked ashen, and was very upset at Ej's behavior, and how shaken I was. I did what I had learned to do. I said I was fine. Just fine. I walked out of the ER to the dark parking lot on shaky knees, and hoped Ej had truly left, and was not waiting there to harm me. I was terrified of my own son.

I also was extremely worried about him. It was so cold. He was so sick. He would need to eat soon, and I had no idea where he would find sustenance. He was walking. It was dark, and dangerous. I went back to my loft, and laid down, but slept very little.

The next day, Evan called and said Ej had contacted him, and wanted to try again.

We were cautious, but we moved forward. We found another pathway, where Ej could participate in an outpatient program. Evan agreed to allow him to move back into his home, and set the following rules: Stay in the program. No drugs. No alcohol. Absolute line in the sand.

Ej agreed, and at first appeared to be succeeding. We worked diligently to help with underlying problems. A van that was essentially abandoned and needing repair. Court issues. Evan and I were finally on the same page, and working towards a new day with our son. We wanted nothing more than for him to progress. We tried.

It was not too many weeks before Ej began to refuse to go to the classes for the inpatient program. I reminded Evan that he had agreed that if Ej dropped his side of the bargain he could no longer stay at his house.

I did that with a weak voice. It was so cold outside, and I could hardly bear to think of my son back on the streets. The stress was beginning to show on Evan, however. He never knew when he returned from working what his home environment would consist of.

A defining day occurred.

Evan found evidence of drug activity and alcohol use in Ej's bedroom. The monster that had invaded our home so many years before had reared its' head once again. Addiction is a terrible monster to battle. So many times, I have thought that as terrifying as it has been for us, it must be tenfold that much more terrifying for our son.

A confrontation occurred. It was ugly. During the course of events, Ej said maybe it was time for him to leave. Evan said maybe that was best. He told him to take whatever he needed, and then to be sure to call and set up a time to come back to get anything else that he wanted to take with him. Ej drove away.

Evan called me that night. It was late. I was up working, and had the immediate sense that something was wrong when my phone rang. I even answered it, asking, "What's the matter?"

Evan shared the story with me. Asked me if I thought he was a bad father. I told him I did not think that at all. I told him to be safe, and go to bed.

I did not sleep well that night. I tossed and turned, and at 6:59am my phone rang the tone that signaled a text message was received.

It was from Evan. It simply said, "Please call when you can."

I immediately knew this was not going to be good news. He thought I would be sleeping, and would not receive the notification until I woke up. I called his number and when he answered I simply said, "What happened?"

He proceeded to explain that in the middle of the night Ej had returned and gotten violent trying to break back into the house. The police arrived, and Ej was once again in custody.

My heart sank. It could not break. It was already in too many pieces.

Evan shared that the police were recommending that he take out a protective order against Ej. Against our son. He tentatively said, "I bet you think that I am the worst dad ever, don't you?"

I said, no. I did not think that. I thought that if we did not do anything to change course, and lost him with an act of violence that would be the worst thing. That too many people loved

271

him and counted on him, and he deserved to be safe, happy, and living his life without fear.

I offered to go with him, if he wanted my support at that hearing. As it turned out, that is exactly what came to pass.

The judge at the hearing was older, and very kind. I sat by Evan's side as he reviewed the facts. Over and over I looked at the paperwork that listed the demographics of the case. Including the birthdates of both Evan and Ej. I kept seeing the date of birth for our son, and wondered again how we had gone from that day of improbability and joy to this one. I was startled out of my deep thoughts when I heard the judge, in a soft voice say, "This is heartbreaking. I can only assume from the names on this case that this is your son. Is that right?"

He then went on to review the facts, and granted the protective order. I walked out of the courtroom and Evan said he needed to sit down. He was emotional, and I sat by his side, unsure what to say or do. We decided to go to a local restaurant for breakfast, but once we arrived there, neither of us could eat very much. It was an overcast, gloomy day, and even though spring was approaching, it appeared to be the end of the world to us. All of our hopes and dreams from the beginning of the year were shattered. Our son was out in the world somewhere, and the old, terrible feeling that he would come to some great harm was ever-present on our minds. We were simply heartbroken.

We left the restaurant, and Evan drove off. I watched until I could no longer see his car, shaking off the old wives tale that it is bad luck to watch someone leave. The familiar ache returned. I knew there was no reason now for him and me to get together, talk, or text. Our mission was officially ended since he no longer could interact with our son.

Work was busy for me. I had multiple clients, and kept myself distracted. The days were growing longer, and the weather was getting warmer. Spring was in the air, but I was sad.

I missed Evan. In addition, I once again felt like a failure as a mother. My son was still lost in the wilderness, and I could do nothing to stop it.

A bright spot that spring was Hannah's graduation from Valencia College in Orlando. She had earned her Associate's degree. Evan and I were ecstatic for her. She was planning to move the weekend after graduation from Orlando back home to Kentucky for the summer., She had been accepted to the University of South Florida to continue her studies and finish her Bachelor's degree the following fall. I called Evan, and suggested we use AirBNB. If we booked a big house together, we could split the costs, and Hannah could stay with us while we packed her apartment.

We decided this was a good approach. I booked the space.

In the weeks leading up to the graduation, the landscape changed. Hannah announced that she had found a job and was going to stay in Orlando after all when the school year ended. We were proud of her work ethic, and secretly sad to not have the time with her at home in Kentucky.

This also meant that her apartment, which was paid for through August, was still in play. As it turned out, Evan and I found ourselves in the AirBNB all alone.

We went to the grocery store together, and fell into a decade's old pattern of helping one another out. When we got back to our condo, we said goodnight and headed to our respective sides of the unit. I awoke the next morning to the smell of bacon cooking. Evan was making breakfast.

It was awesome. It was awkward. We went forward through the next several days, and celebrated Hannah's graduation, and monumental achievement. We met her friends, and shared time with them.

One evening, Evan had plans to go to dinner with a couple he knew. He invited me to join him. I hesitated. I told him I did not want to intrude. He insisted. I went, and it was so easy, and relaxing. It felt right.

We had arrived separately in Orlando for Hannah's graduation. Evan was scheduled to depart a day before I was. The last evening that we were together in the condominium, I opened up to Evan. I said, "Thirty years ago, I would have been charging up a hill, sword drawn, finding the way forward for us. I no longer want that role. I would be so happy to explore this if you want to. However, I need you to let me know what you want. I get it if you do not want to go down this road. I honestly do. I just know that in the almost nine years we have been apart, neither one of us has ever gotten involved with anyone else in any meaningful way. Our young grandchildren think we are married! I do not know what this all means, but I just want you to know that I would be happy to explore this. However, only if you want to as well. I need you to decide, and let me know what you want."

Evan left. The condominium was deafeningly quiet with him gone. I awoke and did not smell bacon cooking for breakfast. I packed, and left feeling as let down as the evening when he had turned me down to go get ready to fish with his father in 1986.

I went back home. I stayed busy. The weather was wonderful, and I returned to my life as an urbanite in downtown Cincinnati. Not long after, Evan called. I was out, eating dinner at one of my favorite downtown places.

He asked, "Where are you?" I responded that I was just around the corner. He asked if he could come and join me. He said he was at a REDS game and was ready to leave. I said of course. He said, "You know we could hang out and NOT talk about any of the kids!" I agreed.

We had a great time, walking, and talking, sharing popcorn and draft beers. We were friends.

The night ended with Evan taking my hand and saying he was considering taking a chance again. Not just with me. Taking a chance on life. On believing that things could be different from what he had resigned himself too.

It became a pattern. I would hear from Evan, and we would do things together. It was so much fun. We had never had the opportunity to be alone together, even from the inception of our relationship. We danced around one another. Neither wanted to overstep, or scare the other one off.

One Friday night, Evan sent a message, asking what I was doing that evening. I told him I was going to a rooftop bar on the Ohio River bank to see a very special friend perform. It was a magical, perfect night. The weather was warm, and soft, and everything felt right. Evan responded that he did not want to intrude. I assured him he was not, took a big leap, and decided to bring a, "date" to see my favorite artist.

Kelsey is a performer, the same age as my children, and simply ridiculously talented. I had started following her a few years before, and as time went along, realized that the couple always in attendance must be her parents. We all became great friends. Other couples our age also followed Kelsey. Everyone was used to me showing up alone.

That evening was different. I showed up with Evan.

It is a hilarious story to recount.

The usual, single seat was saved for me. There were now two of us. Everyone got up, and jostled around to make room for Evan. The minute he walked to the bar to order our drinks every head in the place swung in my direction.

"Who IS he?"

"How did you meet him?"

"The two of you seem VERY comfortable already!"

I dodged and deflected questions. It was later that night that I finally answered truthfully. I said, "Actually, this is the father of my children."

Laughter ensued. I was asked again, who Evan was. I met Kelsey's eyes, and she said, "Oh my gosh!"

She got it. Others did too. Later, Kelsey would explain that she felt so comfortable with my choice and was happy for me.

After that show, Evan walked me back to my loft. He became very quiet at the door. He stalled. I finally asked him what was wrong. Did he forget where he had parked? What he said next changed my life. "I am trying to figure out how to ask for what I want."

That night taught me that second chances do happen.

Evan and I test-drove the waters. We behaved in much the same way as I can image people having an affair do. We drove separately to our grandchildren's events. We just wanted a chance to do this right, on our own. Most of all, we did not want to present ourselves as a couple again to our family, only to say that it was not going to work out.

We had great fun throughout the summer. We cooked dinner. We took long walks across the bridges that spanned the Ohio River. We watched musicians perform. We held hands, and hugged, and just sat together with no need to talk.

It was wonderful. One day, our youngest daughter, Hannah, called. I put her on speaker phone, but did not tell her that her father was listening, and cooking dinner in my kitchen. She asked, "Are you dating Dad?!"

I told her that she needed to just let us alone for a while. That it was private, and I was not ready to talk about it.

Hilariously, after we hung up, Evan's phone rang about ten seconds later. He put it on speaker phone. She asked, "Are you dating Mom?!"

He responded that she just needed to let us alone for a while, that it was private, and he was not ready to talk about it. She almost yelled, "That is what Mom just said!!!"

He then said he knew, because we were together, and he was cooking dinner. Our children had to relearn how to respond to us as a unit. For so many years, they had to go from one of us to the other to get something resolved. This was no longer the case, and it would lead to a learning curve for all of us since our children where now all adults.

My birthday approached. July 4th is actually the perfect birthday for me. My father always called me his firecracker baby. For decades, I had attended the Fourth of July parade through the city of Fort Thomas. My mother and both of my sisters still live there. Evan and I lived there for decades. Before the divorce, Evan and I had always stood at the top of Chalfonte Place, and watched the parade before going to my older sister's house for a cookout. Prior to meeting Evan, I had stood there first as a single young woman, then with Gary, and then on my own as a single mother. This particular summer, I emailed Karen and asked if it would be OK if I brought Evan to the cookout.

For the first time in ten years, Evan was standing by my side. It was such a special day for so many reasons.

The first surprise for me was when the float came by in the parade where Jessica and Kevin's children were riding. Jess and Kevin were walking by the Fort Thomas Education Foundation's float. Jessica had been texting me to let me know I needed to be sure to see them. I kept assuring her I would be there, in the regular place, at the top of the street. I saw their float coming. As it approached, I recognized many of my grandchildren's friends also riding on the float. I saw them often at many soccer and basketball games, and so many other events like plays and fundraisers.

I first remember that flowers were thrown by the children. I turned to Evan, and said, "I wonder what that is for? It looks like what happens to skaters when they are finished with their program!"

I then saw Jessica run from around the back of the float with a neon green sign. It was huge, and proclaimed, Happy Birthday Memaw!

I then realized the flowers were for me. And that the parade had stopped. The children on the float began to sing. "Happy birthday to you! Happy birthday to you! Happy birthday dear (fill in the name, according to who was singing! .....KNOX'S Memaw, or FINLEY'S Memaw, or MARLOWE'S Memaw!!!!!)...happy birthday to you!"

It was so special. The parade took off, and I stood holding the flowers and sign, and felt so blessed.

It was almost as if Evan had never left my side. He fell back into the rituals with my family in such an easy way. He had even asked if the men's bake off contest was still held every year. That was a dessert contest that was judged by the women to decide which man had brought the best dessert to the cookout. Evan announced that he was going to win it.

He spent a long time the evening before preparing his dessert. He won. And I kept shaking my head to figure out what year I was standing in.

A few days later I took the big, green poster to the professional framer in Fort Thomas who had framed all of our artwork for the past thirty years. Ken is friendly and personable. He remarked that the sign was giant, and very, very neon green. I told him I had no idea where I would hang it, but I knew I needed to have it framed.

I then told him that I was thinking of moving back to the Kentucky side of the river. I was missing having a dog, and a house. I was thinking about something else that seemed totally crazy as well. I told Ken I was thinking that maybe Evan and I should move in together. My lease was coming due. It was high time for Evan to move out of his rental property.

Ken looked at me, and said, "Don't forget I am a realtor." He then slid his card across the counter to me.

I started looking at homes for sale on both sides of the river. I found one I wanted to view. I asked Evan to do me a favor and go somewhere with me.

OK. OK. I was doing a mini charging up the mountain with a machete. I could see it so clearly.

We walked through a beautiful home. There was a statue in the yard that was identical to one I had given Evan twenty years before. We thanked Ken, and went to a local restaurant.

I tiptoed forward. I asked what Evan thought about us considering moving in together, and stopping the back and forth we were doing to stay together each night at one of our places. I was uncomfortable staying at his rented home. There were just too many bad memories there, and I worried about our safety.

He said he was not sure. I was a little crestfallen. We left, and I went back to my loft, alone. It was not long before text messages began to pour in. It was Evan, saying he was upset, and unsure why he was so hesitant. He talked about being afraid of actually qualifying to ever own a home again. He said he did not want to be responsible for messing up our new connection.

I assured him that I was OK. I did not want to rush him, or me, into anything. That maybe he was right to be so cautious. That maybe we should just leave things the way they were. It was already pretty great.

The next day, Evan called and said he had thought things through. He wanted to see if he could move. He was very unsure about his ability to buy a house. He had come through a devastating bankruptcy following our divorce. He shared that he had resigned himself to never, ever again owning his own home.

He asked me if I would be disappointed, or upset with him, if we explored this avenue, and found out we could not qualify to do it.

I told him I would not. I would never again regress to anywhere in the past and lose all the progress we had made.

I called Ken. He directed me to his loan officer. I spoke with her, and shared all of our hopes, and fears. She began to work through the process. I asked Evan how he would feel about her running his information to see if he could qualify on his own to purchase a house.

He was skeptical. He agreed, and again asked me if I would be OK if it did not move forward. I was honest, when I said I would be.

It took two days to get an answer. I let myself into Evan's house when I received it. I stopped by the store and picked up his favorite beer and was waiting when he got home. I heard the garage door open, and he walked in a few minutes later. He looked at me, and stopped in his tracks. He assumed if I was there, unexpectedly, it must be bad news.

It was not.

I looked at Evan, and said, "You have a great job. You are stable. You are two years past the end of the bankruptcy. You are prequalified to purchase your own house."

I was unprepared when he began to cry. He finally said, "Let's go find a house."

At this point, the only person I had officially shared that I was even considering doing this with Evan was my mother. I know others suspected, but we had committed to one another to keep this between us until we knew where it would end.

We began to look in earnest at homes both north and south of the Ohio River. Evan put a contract in on a house we thought was perfect in Ohio. We waited by the phone, only to learn that a cash offer had come in, and his had been rejected.

We kept searching. We found a home in Kentucky that we thought looked great. When we visited it, we saw that it needed many repairs, and we were unsure. We drove around the corner, and found a beautiful, perfectly staged, already vacant home. I was sold. Evan was not. He vacillated back and forth between the two.

I told him I would be happy anywhere as long as we were together. That was honest. I did think that he should put in an offer on what we now were referring to as The Gazebo House. The backyard was one I could absolutely see him in, taking care of his bonsai trees.

He continued to lean towards the other house, which had a finished basement. He told me his choice. I was honest when I said I would be happy there. We hung up that night. Six or seven hours later my phone rang.

Evan said, "You are going to think I am crazy, but I am back to thinking about putting in a contract on The Gazebo House."

I remember saying, "I KNOW! RIGHT!"

Evan placed the bid. It was accepted. We were under contract.

The usual bumps happened along the way. We waited until we were through the house inspection before we told anyone about our crazy plans. I shared with my oldest, Jessica, after I was sure that it was all going to go through. She shocked me when she immediately began to cry. I said, "I thought this would be good news."

She replied, "It is."

A few days later, she showed up with a customized Christmas ornament that had the address stenciled on it. A new beginning!

As the summer wound down, we found ourselves again traveling to Florida. This time, we were helping our daughter, Hannah, move from Orlando, and the school she had just graduated from to Tampa, to begin her work in Deaf Studies at The University of South Florida. Once again, we had reserved an AirBNB and split the costs. We worked through torrential rainstorms, but finally got Hannah settled in her new place.

One evening, Hannah was out with her friends. Evan and I were at a local restaurant and were enjoying dinner. I honestly do not remember which one of us said it first. Eventually the subject of getting remarried surfaced.

I assured Evan that I would not be moving in with him if my commitment was not the same as if we married. I told him how happy I would be if the same minister could marry us again. I shared with Evan that we should try and book Kelsey for a private event. He agreed that would be so special.

I had kept in touch with the minister who married us through social media. Gerald had married Evan and I in 1988, baptized our children, and then moved to California about fifteen years before to pastor a church in California. His wife, Tammy, who we loved, had died of cancer years before. I remembered sitting in my office in West Virginia, at that time, watching the memorial service that was streaming from California, and thinking that the whole world had gone mad.

During the funeral service, Gerald shared a story that remained with me. He spoke about being out, walking and trying to make sense of the fact that his wife was apparently going to die, leaving him and their three children. The sky above him was an ominous, dark color, and looked as if it would storm at any second. He looked up at a mountain range, and saw that just beyond the highest peak of the mountain, the sky had cleared, and sun was breaking through on the other side. Gerald felt as if it were a message from God. There are dark, scary, ominous times, but just beyond the peak, the sun will shine again.

I had been in touch with Gerald to ask for his prayers as we worked to help our son. As the months went along, I sent him a message that spoke about Evan and I attempting to pick up the pieces again and move ahead with our relationship.

After the discussion in the restaurant with Evan in Tampa, I communicated to Gerald that we were considering being remarried. I was asking how we might get together across the miles and have Gerald remarry us. To ask if he even would consider it, as I knew he took his responsibility in marrying couples very seriously.

He sent a message back, asking what number, and time would be best for him to call. I set up a time for the following Monday, after our return home from Tampa.

Evan headed to work that day, and right on time, Gerald called my phone. We talked a while, just catching up voice to voice versus messaging. I asked him what he thought about our idea. How I was unsure that we could ever get all of our family to him on the west coast. I asked if he ever came back to Kentucky for any reason.

He quietly said, "You know I have not been to Kentucky in a few years, but my wife, Gesa and I are headed that way at the end of next week. If we back up our flights one day, I could perform the marriage on September 8th."

I remember choking out, "You mean 2017?" He laughed at me, and said yes, September 8th, 2017. We hung up, with Gerald promising to check to see what it would cost to change their flights. I texted Evan. He texted back that he was ready, but was it even possible? We both had to turn in the keys to our respective homes by the end of August. We were in full-blown moving mode, essentially a double move, first my loft, and then his house.

I said, I thought it could be done. I mean, why not?

He agreed, and I began to witness divine intervention occur. It was one of the rare times in my life where I was in exactly the right place, doing exactly what I was supposed to be doing, in alignment with my moral compass and dreams. God showed up.

My phone rang again. Gerald excitedly shared that there was not going to be a change fee of any kind to back he and Gesa's tickets up to the flight one day earlier. The reason? There is a waiver of change fees if the airline alters the details of the purchased flight in any way. Their original flight's departure time had been moved by a few minutes. Which qualified them for the waiver.

I said, "That is terrific! Let's do it!"

I then hung up, and called a private club I belonged to, a beautiful place, called The Metropolitan Club. Normally, private events need to be booked well in advance, especially on weekends, because it is very popular. I asked, "Is there any chance that any of the private rooms are open a week from Friday? I am getting married, and was hoping there might be a small space still available there that we might use."

The response? "Dr. Luse, we were just talking about that this morning. For some reason, next Friday is wide open. The entire side is available, so we could push back the dividing walls and you can have the whole space if you like. We have a manager of events, named Sydney, who will work with you. We can handle the ceremony, the food, the bar, and the cake."

I said, "That is terrific! Let's do it!"

I sent Kelsey a text. I had asked her to learn a song for me about a month back, so I could dance to it with Evan. The song was, "The Story of My Life" by Neil Diamond. The text read, "Hey Kelsey, are you performing anywhere on Friday, September 8th?"

She responded that she had a gig at the Kenwood Country Club, but might be able to switch with another band if I knew of an opportunity that night that she should look at.

I responded that I wanted her to sing, "The Story of My Life" at my wedding that night.

Initially, she thought it was a joke. And then came another text: "OH MY GOSH!" She and her wonderful family went into high gear to rearrange things so that they could be with us.

I said, "That is terrific! Let's do it!"

I then called the local florist that we had used for decades. My friends at Fort Thomas Florist told me they were already double-booked for the weekend. They asked what the occasion was. I told them that Evan and I were going to remarry. They told me they would figure it out, and make sure they could provide the flowers for us.

I said, "That is terrific! Let's do it!"

So, in the span of about two hours, the venue, the minister, the entertainment, the flowers, and the catering was all secured. I then thought about what I could possibly wear. My mind returned to all the boxes that were laying around my loft. I tentatively pulled out one that was a bit battered, and discolored, and sealed shut.

I carefully cut the tape and took the top off the box. Inside lay my wedding dress from 1988. A beautiful, pale pink gown, that had been cleaned and preserved nearly three decades before.

I stepped into it, hoping that all the work I had invested in reclaiming my life and waistline over the past year had paid off. I pulled the zipper up. It would work!

I made another call, this time to the local alterations specialist that I trust. I said, "Frances, I know that you are always booked out, but could you possibly cut a train off of a special dress for me?"

She responded, "I just had someone cancel tonight at 6pm. If you bring it in, I can get that done for you. What is the special occasion?"

I told her, and she was excited. I ended that evening standing on the platform in the middle of her shop as she pinned the hemline. I asked her if she thought it was appropriate for me to wear the dress now that I was so much older than the first time. She said she thought it was beautiful.

I then texted our family and told them that they needed to clear their calendars, and join Evan and I on September 8th. Jessica called, and asked about the details. When I told her about wearing my pink dress, she said, "Hey, do you still have my pink dress from your first wedding?" I was not connecting the dots. I told her I was sure that it would be far too small for her, since she was just three the first time around. She helped me understand when she responded, "Mom! Finley could wear it!"

I misted over thinking about the beautiful life circle where my granddaughter would be standing with us in the same dress that her mother wore all those years ago. With all of my moving, and all of the changes, I had taken the pictures, dresses, video, and every memento from 1988 with me. I still had everything.

Evan came home shortly afterwards and asked what I had been doing all day. I told him I hoped he was serious about the wedding discussion. Because it was on! He smiled, and we embraced, and began to appreciate exactly how miraculous it was.

A few days later we went to church. We were just five days from our wedding day. One of our friends walked up after the service and said, "Anyone who doesn't believe in the power of God should stand here and watch the two of you holding hands, singing, after all that has happened."

We met just once with Sydney at The Metropolitan Club to discuss logistics and menu options. We placed everything into her capable hands. We had one FaceTime session with Gerald to talk about things overall. He had some wise advice for us, recommending that we eliminate any people in our lives that could not get behind us and be supportive. He said he would work on the ceremony. We knew it would be meaningful. Gerald was part of the tapestry of our lives.

A few days later, I went back to see Frances. The dress was hemmed to perfection. I stood there, looking into the mirror, and asked one more time...."Frances, tell me the truth. If you were at the wedding this Friday, and saw me walk in wearing this, would you think I was crazy?"

She covered her mouth with both hands, and slowly shook her head up and down. Yes? Yes! Yes, she would think I was crazy!

I teared up. She stepped back. She then said the most hysterical thing. "Kim, it is those God-awful eighties sleeves. Now that you don't have gigantic eighties hair, your head looks like the size of a pin!"

She turned around and picked up a razor blade, and instructed me to hold my arms out to the sides, and trust her.

Trust her? She was cutting off my sleeve, while I was wearing it!

It didn't take very long. The enormous, flouncy sleeve fell to the floor. About that time, a woman knocked on the back door, entered, delivering supplies to the shop. Frances asked her, "Hey, do you like this dress with the big sleeve on, or the sleeve cut off?" I was standing there modeling one sleeve on, one sleeve off.

Without missing a beat, the woman I had never met pointed to the arm that was bare. She then said, "The other one? Totally eighties!"

We all laughed, and Frances told me to take the dress off, and leave it for one more day. She would remove the other sleeve without me wearing it while she was using a razor blade.

Everything began to move very quickly, and I began to make lists. Pick up the dress. Check. Meet with Kelsey. Check. Pick up Evan's tuxedo. Check.

We then realized we did not have anyone earmarked to take pictures. Evan offered that his landlord, who was coming to the wedding with his wife, had been taking photography classes. One text later, Mark had agreed to serve as the photographer of record to capture our reunion.

In 1988, we had a very large video recorder, that Evan's brother used to videotape our ceremony. We decided we would show the beginning of that wedding, and when it was stopped, begin again with our new ceremony. Evan seemed incredulous that I still had the old recording. At one point, in years past, I actually had the VHS tape transferred to a CD to prevent further deterioration.

Everything was set. The day of the wedding arrived. Evan and I woke up together that morning in our new home, boxes everywhere. We kept laughing about how it was so different than the first time, where we carefully made sure to not see one another the day of the wedding before the ceremony, and had so many little ones to attend to. The weather was perfect. We got ready, and headed to The Metropolitan Club.

We arrived to find Kelsey practicing our song. It was a little surreal. The sky was the perfect shade of blue, and the space looked beautiful. The flowers had been delivered. I looked twice at my bouquet and saw that a piece of the fabric from my sleeves was tied around the stems. Evan and I had decided we would walk up the aisle together this time, only asking for our two young granddaughters to walk up first, dropping rose petals. I looked at the baskets, and realized they were also made out of my gigantic sleeves. I was told that was a surprise from Frances. She knew the florists well, and went down after I picked up my dress, and covered the baskets with the left over fabric.

We took photos. We laughed. I was so relaxed, and at one point, Mark said it was a shame that we had not taken any photos outside on such a

beautiful day. Sydney said we could go out
between the buildings, stand on chairs, and take
photos with the Ohio River and the Cincinnati
skyline as our backdrop. It worked so well.
Towards the end, I looked up, and saw Jessica
and Kevin, and their three beautiful children, as
well as Hannah standing in the doorway. I
motioned them to join us, and the children burst
through the doors. Finley wearing Jessica's
dress from 1988. Marlowe dressed in a
beautiful pink dress as well. Knox was carrying a
pillow. Jessica said that once she told him about
the wedding, he asked if he could be the ring
bearer, since he had done that the year before
for close friends of their family. We took more
pictures, and as we began to head into the
building again I looked up. Gerald and Gesa
were headed towards us.

We had not seen Gerald for years. It was so
good to see him again, and meet his new wife.
We all headed upstairs. The rest of our children
began to arrive. Before long, it was time to
begin.

We decided I would stand in the control room
with Sydney so I could let her know the exact
point to stop the video of our first wedding. I
heard Gerald get up, welcome the group, and
share that this was a celebration that had begun

29 years ago. He motioned to the video screen. Everything seemed to be going perfectly.

Until Sydney and I looked down and saw the computer powering itself down for an update. The video was not going to play like that!

I felt my heart start to pound. Sydney was completely calm. Dropped to her knees in her beautiful suit and began making sure all the connections were secure and everything was plugged in. I had to power everything up. Murmurs began to go through the audience. Gerald appeared in the doorway, and asked what was happening. I heard myself saying, "They've waited almost nine years, everyone can wait a few more minutes!"

Mercifully, the computer powered back up. The video began. I calmed my breathing, and wondered why I had not written down my vows. I then looked up towards the sky and said a prayer to remember that no matter what happened, I was blessed to be there. Everything would be fine.

I heard the familiar song, "Somewhere Out There" begin to play on the video. We played the ceremony through that song, and past Gerald's first remarks, and then stopped it when Gerald announced all those years ago, "The

woman you love is about to become your wife"
I joined Evan at the back of the parlor. Kelsey
began to sing, "Somewhere Out There" to begin
our second trip down the aisle.

Gerald headed down first, signaling that the
ceremony was about to begin. Finley headed
down, dropping rose petals from the basket
made from the sleeve of my gown, wearing her
mother's dress from 29 years before.

Marlowe, usually fearless, took a few tentative
steps, and then did a large U-turn. She walked
straight back to me, and said, in all earnestness,
"I NO do this, Memaw!" She looked frightened.

I picked our two-year-old granddaughter up, and
said, "You don't have to do this." Evan and I,
and Marlowe headed up the aisle together. At
the front, I handed her to her mother, and we
turned to face Gerald.

He began by offering a prayer: *God—Because of
your great love for us, we're gathered here to
celebrate love. We celebrate the love that Evan
has for Kimberly and that Kimberly has for Evan.*

*We ask You God, to move this event from just a
wedding day to a spiritual day; from secular to
sacred; from human to divine. In that way, as we
witness their love for each other, we will be*

touched by Your great love, as well. Amen.

The remarks that followed were meaningful. Gerald knew our story from the beginning. He jokingly referred to our wedding that evening as version 2.0, leading us to always refer to it that way. He had spoken with Kelsey prior to the ceremony, so when it became time for her to sing our song, "The Story of My Life" he preceded it with a request. He asked for all of our children, their spouses, and significant others, and all of our grandchildren to come forward and stand behind and with us.

It was a large group, and again I was struck by the meaningfulness of our union, and how many lives it directly affected. Gerald said, "Kimberly and Evan, the people standing here with you, and those in this room, represent the story of your life to this point." Kelsey began to sing. I turned and began to hug everyone. Evan did the same.

After the song, another prayer was offered: Well, with that support, let's pray together. *Father, thank you for the significance of this moment and the importance of their children and their families standing here, pledging their support to Evan and Kimberly. Each of them is your gift to this couple. I thank you for them and the fullness of life that they bring. We also acknowledge that there's a son and grandson missing from this circle. And so even today we ask for your protection for EJ and Cassady, along with healing and hope for the day when EJ will return to his place in this family. Thank you for the support that those here have pledged for the union of this couple and may your richest blessings rest on each of them and all of them. Amen.*

It has been a balancing act for Evan and me, to help everyone in our lives understand how much we love them, and to also acknowledge that there is a void, with the absence of our son, and the limited time we get to spend with his son, our grandson Cassady. We were happy to have them included in Gerald's prayer for intercession and protection.

We had decided to write our own vows to one another. Evan began, and his remarks were so touching. The most meaningful thing he said was that he pledged to stand beside me when I needed his help, and to step aside when I didn't. He had learned the secret to loving a strong, independent woman.

I shared with him my deep admiration for his abiding faith, and the fact that everything just is better for me when he is here. That I knew that never again would I feel that terrible ache in my stomach as we parted ways after one of the grandchildren's games, walking in different directions, to separate cars. We were together again. After all of the years of moving, and heartache, I was finally, truly home.

The rest of the evening was such a celebration. Each day that I wake up, I again thank God for the miracle that has brought us back together. It is a union I will protect every day for the rest of the days I have left in my lifetime. I do not know what the future has in store, but I know that I believe the answer I received when I asked Evan if he thought a future crisis would tear us back apart. He calmly said, "No matter what happens, we are better together." That's enough for me.

Lessons learned?

- Family is everything. Everything else is just everything else.
- There is no price too high to pay for behaving in an ethical manner.
- If you find yourself outside of the circle, make your own circle, and invite others in.
- Everybody wets his or her pants at some point.
- Do not play jax if you really want to run a foot race instead.

- You do not have to have all of the answers.
- Trust the universe. Follow the path.
- You will never find true happiness if you are not in alignment with your moral compass.
- Being a parent is a blessing.
- No one will ever be as happy to see you as your grandchildren.
- At the end of the day, it is important that you have treated others well.
- Forgive those who have hurt you.
- Ask for forgiveness when you have hurt others.
- Nobody is perfect.
- Life is a gift.
- When you are in a dark place, know that the morning is coming.

To contact Kimberly Luse, visit www.strategicethicalsolutions.com, or email Kimberly@strategicethicalsolutions.com. Services provided include public speaking, executive coaching, professional development, and strategic planning.

Made in the USA
Monee, IL
14 August 2020